Rainbow's End

A Parent's Guide To Understanding Transsexual Children and Teens

Kay Brown

DEDICATION

To my loving husband, Jeff

CONTENTS

INTRODUCTION

As an adoptive and foster parent myself, please allow me to express that you have my most sincere empathy. Being a parent isn't easy. Raising children is both a privilege and sacred trust. You are entrusted with the well-being and responsibility to support another human being as they become an adult who will stand on their own. Your job is helping them become the best person that they rightfully are, whatever that may be.

You are also charged with protecting your child. Since much of the advice I give here may not be found anywhere else, you need to know it. As a transsexual child and teen, I would have loved for my parents to have known this material. This material is not theoretical. Many of the issues I list below happened to me, my friends, and my charges. I was an unhappy and lonely child, described by my mother as "prissy" and girlish, beginning as a toddler, put into play therapy when I was ten, again 'talk' therapy when I was 15/16, and fortunately for me, was formally diagnosed as transsexual at the age of 17, at the then newly formed Stanford Gender Dysphoria Clinic, in early 1975. I "came out" in high school around the same time and have lived happily as a girl/woman, wife, and mother since then. In addition to my own personal experiences growing up, I was a foster-mother to two girls, one a very gender atypical girl, now lesbian, the other I officially adopted... and "unofficial" foster mother / god mother to several transkids, when they were teens through young adult. I also served as a Court Appointed Special Advocate (CASA) for an FtM transkid in foster care who is now an adult.

1 PARENTAL ANGST

You may be asking yourself, "Why *my* child?" or "What did we do *wrong*?"

You did nothing wrong, and there is nothing you could have done, nor do now, to prevent or change your child's nature. While we don't know exactly what causes a child to be gender atypical and dysphoric, we do know that it is in-born, biologically determined, before birth, with hints that it is partly genetic, and partly caused by prenatal uterine biological environment factors. Nothing you could have said, or done, would have changed this outcome. Your child does not blame you. Nothing you do now will change the ultimate outcome, save that denial, emotional rejection, or abandonment will deeply harm your relationship with your child; while loving support will deepen it.

It is common for parents, when they first learn from their child that they are gender dysphoric to be in denial. They may have searched the web for 'proof' that their child is not "transgendered". They will read propaganda from militantly anti-LGBT religious groups or "gender skeptical" parents. Or they may focus on activities that their child did (often with parental encouragement or even insistence) that were not gender atypical. They may say, *"My child is just confused, this is just a phase, teenage drama, it will blow over."*

"Denial will not serve. You will win some battles, but lose the war."

Dr. Norman Fisk, early pioneer in transsexual research, who coined the term, "gender dysphoria", offered this advice to the father of a 17-year-old MTF transkid back in early '75, telling him he should be supportive of that teen's efforts to socially transition to living as a girl and get medical help, rather than continue his obstructionism, saying, *"Denial will not serve. You will win some battles, but lose the war."* (That father, of course, was mine...)

Some parents attempt to "fix" their transkids by sending them to therapists (mine certainly did). But there has never been ANY properly controlled study that shows that it is possible to make someone be non-transgendered or transsexual, or to keep someone from becoming transgendered or transsexual. There have been some therapists who have made claims regarding their successes of "curing" transsexual children, but given that most gender atypical young children naturally "grow out of it" by the time they are ten to thirteen years old, these therapists are wrongly claiming credit for what is a naturally occurring process. In a few cases, these therapists claimed "cures" which were later shown to have been merely the children telling the therapist what they wanted to hear.

Some of these therapeutic regimes are emotionally abusive, which in effect, tell children and teens that they are defective in some fashion. Because of this, a few states have now passed, or are considering, laws that prohibit these "conversion" or "reparative" therapies.

You may be worried, even fearful, for your child's future. It is common for parents of transkids to worry that their child will have trouble with jobs and careers, that no one will hire them. Another fear is that they will never have a loving spouse. Or you may be sad that your child will never have children of their own. I can tell you from having known literally dozens of adult former transkids, that we do get jobs, have meaningful careers, find loving partners... and a few of us have been blazing trails in adoption and other alternative family planning options. Nothing is guaranteed in life, but I can tell you that your child has every hope of having a very good and happy life.

As the parent of a gender atypical child, you likely have gotten comments from ignorant and insensitive people who have made ugly remarks about your child, and even of your parenting skills. You may be embarrassed by your child at times. You may wish that they would change and be "normal". But remember, your child didn't "decide" to be gender atypical, s/he just is.

Still, you may also be feeling sad, a sense of loss for the child you hoped you would be raising. This is expected and normal. You may also find that there are times that you are angry, angry with the universe, with life, with your child... With time, this too shall pass.

Raising children is a sacred trust. Gender atypical children are not a burden, they are a blessing to be celebrated.

Educating yourself

It can be very confusing when first learning about transgender experiences. Of course, I recommend reading my own pages here if you want to understand more of the science, but that isn't, strictly speaking, necessary. Instead, there are several excellent books about parenting transkid children and teenagers. But be very, very cautious about reading about transgender and transsexuality in general, especially personal websites. Most of it is about <u>autogynephilic</u> transgender identity and experience; most especially, don't waste your time reading autobiographies of late transitioning (full adult) MTF transsexuals. These will not apply to your child, and reading them will only cause confusion.

You will also learn about the so-called "Standards of Care", which unfortunately have, over the years, been instituted to guide health care providers in helping adult transitioning MTF transsexuals. Although these SOC's have gotten better in recent years, they in some ways are still inappropriate for transkids.

In the English speaking nations, MTF transsexuals who were transkids or "sissy boys" are a small minority among transsexual adults. Most MTF transsexuals transitioned as adults, typically around age 30 to 40, but some as old as their 70's. But adult transitioning MTF transsexuals have a completely different biological etiology (medical condition / cause) and experience than transkids, being autogynephilic and gender *typical*, masculine — even hypermasculine (think: "Navy Seal" or "Olympic champion") as boys and young men. Learning about them can be eye-opening, but will not aid you in understanding your transgendered child.

Adult FtM transsexuals on the other hand were nearly all transkids or "tomboys", though a small number weren't.

It is unfortunate that the two separate conditions that give rise to MTF of a transkid, have been unwittingly thrust into a position where you must learn enough of both so that you may distinguish between the two, so that you may know what will be helpful to your child, and what won't.

If, as you learn more about transgender experience and issues, you become aware of the differences between transkids and adult transitioning transsexuals, you may become profoundly aware that your child's experiences are NOT those of adult MTF transsexuals. You may then wish to become a true activist / advocate. If so, you may wish to further your education by reading the scientific literature on the subject. I sincerely hope you will speak up and educate other parents and health care workers of the differences and special needs of transkids.

Getting help and support for yourself

Take care of yourself. Parenting is often challenging at the best of times. But any parent of an atypical child, whether it be because they have health issues, disabilities, or emotional challenges will experience additional stress. Be sure to cultivate a support network of friends and family.

You are not alone. There are a number of organizations of parents of gender non-conforming children and teens, as well as individuals that support such parents.

Be aware that there are older autogynephilic MTF transsexuals who also belong to these organizations and that many are in denial about their etiology and sexuality, often having edited their history to seem more like transkids. Meeting them, you may become concerned that your child is similar. Be assured that they do not represent your child's future. Also, be aware that parents and wives of autogynephilic MTF transsexuals may offer advice that makes no sense for your transkid. At the present time, awareness and understanding of the special needs of transkids is deplorably absent.

2 SHAMEFUL HISTORY

There is an ongoing 'war of words' concerning the best course of treatment for gender atypical & dysphoric youth. Lately, as our society has learned to accept and even celebrate LGBT youth, there has been a reaction from religious and reactionary bigots who would wish to return to the days when parents and medical caregivers could treat gender atypicality as a serious psychiatric disorder that needed drastic interventions in and of itself, rather than a non-pathological variance found in all human societies. So, perhaps it is time to review the history of such interventions in the light of more recent scientific and humanitarian knowledge.

First, one must understand that historically, gender atypicality concerns were mostly focused on male children, 'sissies'. It was often assumed that 'tomboys' would outgrow it, but sissy boys would all too likely (and statistics bear this out) grow up to be homosexual or transsexual, both equally considered as disordered, criminal, and to be avoided at all costs.

To understand the nature of a given intervention one must first understand the underlying assumptions about the etiology of gender atypicality, dysphoria, and sexual orientation that a given intervention was designed to address. During the mid-20th Century several competing theories vied with each other but there was a common thread, that of a disturbance of nurture. That is to say, that they rejected the role of biology and focused on the environment. So, if the environment is broken, so will the child be. From there, several theories emerge, first up, faulty family constellation, lack of "appropriate" role modeling, and the "Smother Mother".

The faulty family constellation theory is from observations that many children grow up in so-called "broken homes", where single mothers are raising children on her own, with no man in her life. The theory is that a boy child simply has no male role model and thus learns only feminine behavior and identification. But, this wasn't true of all feminine boys. So, another term was added, the "emotionally absent" father. This was a man, who though physically present in the home, rejected his son and thus failed to mold the young boy's behavior toward the "healthy" masculine norm. Of course, a modern understanding would be that the boy's femininity had been the cause of the rejection by a homophobic father, not the other way around. Also, many masculine heterosexual boys had grown up in single mother households, so they had to add the term "vulnerable" to the description of the boys, that is to say, only those who were "vulnerable" to this absence developed into sissies.

The theory also holds that the mother in these families tends to 'smother' a boy, hold him close to her body for excessively long periods, 'tie him to her apron strings', etc., such that he can't form a separate gender identity, or even any identity, of his own.

The intervention designed to 'fix' the faulty family constellation is to introduce a "healthy" masculine heterosexual male role model to the boy and encourage identification and subsequent modeling upon that man. Since it isn't always practical to require a single mother to find a suitable husband willing to take on the task of 'toughening up' the sissy boy, the goal is to place the boy in therapy sessions with a suitable role modeling therapist. For a pre-teen this would often mean "play therapy" with sex typed boys toys. Ideally, there would also be family therapy where the boy's father would be encouraged to take a greater role in the child's upbringing and similar withdrawal of the mother's involvement. Playing with girl's toys is to be actively denied and punished, taking away beloved toys and dolls, often lampooned as "Drop the Barby" therapy. Another aspect would be to restrict the boy from having female friends and require them to participate in single sex activities such as scouting, etc. where they are often exposed to peer disapproval and even bullying, as a means of providing negative (aversive) "natural consequences" to their feminine demeanor. It sounds almost gentle and acceptable (compared to electro-shock or emetic drugs then in use in adults)... but underneath, the message to the child is that they are not "ok", that there is something deeply wrong with them, that they are not lovable as they are, leading to reduced self-esteem and increased loneliness.

While we can all applaud the idea of family intervention to encourage more paternal involvement and bonding, the idea of decreased maternal involvement is simply not justified given that we now know that the faulty family constellation theory is just plain bogus. Further, if a homophobic father can't step up and bond with a feminine boy, that boy will need his mother's acceptance all the more. Further, placing the blame upon the mother for having "encouraged" the boy's femininity in this manner is just plain evil.

{Personal Note: At the age of ten, during the '67-'68 school year, I was sent to such "play therapy" with Dr. Peters (you can't make this stuff up), a tall bearded man in a large room filled with toys. I don't remember seeing any girl's toys in the room, ever. According to my parents, separately, since they divorced when I was a teen, I trust that they were both being candid with me, it had been the school psychologist who had insisted that I be referred to Dr. Peters and only Dr. Peters. This would also explain why my teachers interfered with my female friendships and forced me to interact with boys in class, and there was nothing subtle about it, why I was required to join the Scouts where I hated by the boys, harassed, bullied, brutally beaten, and eventually kicked out by the Scout Master, sneeringly, as "not Eagle Scout Material". My father was mortified! — What I find saddening about the episode is that in my case, the faulty family constellation theory is completely reversed. My mother, though an amazingly capable and caring parent, was the one who became emotionally unavailable and rejecting. It was my good fortune that my Dad was always a very warm, loving, caring, and devoted father to all four of his children... though, if we are all honest about it, I was likely his favorite.}

Another intervention that gained some currency in the mid to late 20th Century is, in effect, to place a child into a Skinner Box, that is to say, create a deliberate reward & punishment system, in therapy, in the home, and in the classroom, in which gender typical behavior is consistently recognized and rewarded, perhaps with tokens redeemable for desirable privileges, while gender atypical behavior is penalized. This type of environment is often used in cases of extremely "disturbed", aggressive, or violent children and teens where cooperative behavior is rewarded and aggression is penalized. Here, the theory is that child is held to be "gender disturbed", expanding the definition used for one class of children requiring extraordinarily harsh and controlling interventions to another. There were a number of 'therapist / researchers' who have published and recommended such interventions using just this pathologizing language.

One of these, George Rekers, a self-hating closeted gay man, not content to label gender atypical boys "disturbed", not satisfied with the stigmatizing term "effeminate" boy, coined the even more powerfully pathologizing and stigmatizing term "feminoid" in the manner of the racist stigmatizing of those with Down's Syndrome as "mongoloid". One of Reker's recommendations included abusively "spanking" (beating actually) young feminine boys when they committed some feminine behavioral infraction. Interestingly, Rekers own research showed that such feminine boys were essentially like gender typical girls,

"The amount of feminine play by the feminoid boys was found to be significantly greater than that of normal boys, but not significantly different from the predominantly feminine play patterns of the normal girls."

Imagine putting a gender typical girl through this... yes, that's the moral and psychological equivalent. I can't even begin to express how evil I find this so-called "therapy". And this is what some parents and pundits wish us to resume?

Special Note:

One of the most important and yet at the same time, distressing aspects of this shameful history is that these abusive interventions came out of the University of California Los Angeles (UCLA) in the late '60s and '70s. It is important to understand that at the beginning of this program, they believed that they were treating transsexual children and had not yet realized that many of these boys would grow up to be gay men. At the very heart and center of this was Robert Stoller and Richard Green. It was Dr. Green who gathered together these vulnerable gender atypical children to allow graduate students to conduct this shameful "research". Rekers, in his published paper on the "treatment" (read: torture) of Kirk Murphy (aka Kraig), thanks Dr. Green for providing him his victim. Further, Dr. Green was personally involved in the research. Knowing this has certainly lowered my esteem for Dr. Green who I had previously held in high regard.

Interestingly, the journal that originally published Reker's key paper describing this horrific 'treatment protocol' has flagged the paper as problematic and of dubious value.

3 THE TYPES OF TRANSSEXUALS

There are two basic biological taxons (types) with their own unique etiologies (causes / conditions) that are found in transsexuals / transgendered people. They are mutually exclusive and distinct. That is to say, one and only one of these two conditions can be found in any one person, there is no overlap or blending between them. The conditions, and those people with them, only superficially resemble each other but are often confused and conflated with each other in the media, by the general public, and even by transfolk themselves. That is to say, that there are two, and only two, separate "transgender spectrums".

This is NOT like thinking of the two types as being the difference between a Pekinese and a Great Dane. The difference between these is "dimensional". Yes, they are different, but they are still the same species, both dogs... and dogs come in many sizes and shapes, but still all dogs.

Think of these two types of transsexuals / transgenders as being separate species, perhaps like dogs and cats. They both run on four legs, are covered in fur, have the same number of claws, prefer to eat meat, make good pets, love being petted, both deserve to be treated well, etc. Yet, for all of their similarities, they are NOT the same animal. And while a Pekinese is the same size as a house cat, you wouldn't confuse the two. Think: Laverne Cox vs. Caitlyn Jenner. Think: *Pose* vs. *TransParent.*

Just as with cats and dogs, both types of transsexual/transgendered people deserve to be treated well; both equally deserve legal, social, and medical recognition as the gender to which they identify and aspire.

One, often thought of as the "classic" pattern, the one that is most familiar in the public understanding, is *extremely gender atypical* from early childhood, often gender dysphoric from preschool age onward, and universally and exclusively attracted to their same natal sex (opposite of their gender identity) when they reach their teens and beyond. They have unstudied mannerisms and social behavior that more closely hews to those found in the other sex. They find their sexed body deeply repugnant and embarrassing from an early age, but increasingly so at puberty. Their cross-sex gender identity and decision to transition come early in life and feels like an easy and natural extension of their previous history. Unlike the other type, they do **not** experience sexual arousal with cross-dressing or to the thought of being or becoming the opposite sex.

Transsexuals with this etiology are most often called, "early onset" or "homosexual transsexuals" (HSTS) in the scientific literature. (This does **not** imply that they act like, nor identify, as gay or lesbian. It only means that they are sexually and affectionally attracted to gender typical members of the same natal sex. This term is very often considered offensive by the very people it describes and should only be used in scientific papers and discussions, if at all.) They are sometimes called "transgender children", "transkids", or "transgendered youth" (transyouth) in common parlance. As adults they may be called "former transkids". In this book, I call them "transsexual"

There are some differences in life arcs of Female-to-Male (FtM) and Male-To-Female (MTF) transkids. The median age of transition for MTF of this type is 20 years old, with a range of early puberty to mid 20's. More than 95% transition full time before the age of 25 and it is unheard of to find one who transitions full time after age 30. The median age of transition for FtMs is slightly older, with a moderate number transitioning in their 30's and later, usually after having attempted to live as very butch (masculine) lesbians. Thinking about transkids as individuals who are so like the opposite sex that they might as well be that sex offers a straight forward and insightful way of viewing these kids.

The other type is generally *gender typical* in behavior as a child, adolescent, and into early adulthood, but may experience transient gender dysphoria, none the less, usually kept secret, due to shame. (Note: These children, teenagers, and adults are hiding their *desire* to be, or be like, the other sex, *not* gender atypical behavior, which they don't naturally have.) Their cross-gender identity takes time to develop and solidify as the process is often quite emotionally distressing, confusing, and vacillating. They are mostly attracted to the opposite natal sex and to other transgendered people, especially to early onset transsexuals (who universally are NOT interested in return), but may be behaviorally bisexual or asexual. They exhibit an unusual sexual arousal pattern, a particular sexual orientation, usually called an *Erotic Target Location Error* in the scientific literature, in which they map their preferred sexual object, the opposite sex, onto their own bodies and actions, and thus find the thought of being or becoming the opposite sex to be arousing and emotionally rewarding, leading to an *Erotic Target Identity Inversion*, in which they come to identify as a member of the class of people to which they are attracted, specifically, the opposite sex. They may also find altering their appearance to approximate the opposite sex, by cross-dressing, to also be sexually arousing and emotionally rewarding. In Female-to-Male (FtM) transgendered individuals, it is called "autoandrophilia" (AAP) and in Male-To-Female (MTF) transgendered individuals this arousal pattern is called "autogynephilia" (AGP). (When refering to both autoandrophilia and autogynephilia "A*P" may be used.) Transsexuals with this etiology are most often called, "non-homosexual transsexuals" or "late onset" in the scientific literature.

Before transition, the natural behavior of late-onset / non-homosexual / autogynephilic MTF transsexuals is gender typical, easily passing as typical straight men, often marrying women, fathering children, and successful in stereotypically masculine and even hyper-masculine (e.g. Navy Seal) careers. It is not uncommon for them to exhibit homophobic and sexist attitudes. As it can take years for the cross-gender identity to form and establish itself, the modal age for transition is 35 to 40 years old, the mean is between 40 to 45, with a range of early 20's to very old age. They are far more likely to transition in individualistic cultures than socially interdependent cultures. After transition, they may identify as lesbian, asexual/uncertain, bisexual, or even straight women, including marrying men. Thinking about autogynephilic MTF transsexuals as "male bodied people who love women and (romantically) want to become what they love" offers a more accurate and more richly informative way to understand them.

Before transition, the natural behavior of non-homosexual / autoandrophilic FtM may be quite variable, but is usually less "butch" than exclusively gynephilic FtM transsexuals. Their families would likely describe them as having been very typical girls, with some tomboyish interests, comfortable being feminine (dresses, make-up, nail polish, etc.). Their sexuality is most likely to be also variable over time, where they may find men or women more attractive as partners at different times in their lives. Overt erotic cross-dressing occurs only rarely, but other aspects of autoandrophilia may be found in their fantasy life (e.g. erotic interest in <u>Yaoi Manga</u> and/or M/M Alpha/Omega novels) or having crushes on FtM transkids. We know less about such transmen as we do autogynephilic transwomen, but that is changing rapidly.

Because of the difference in mean age at transition, the first type is often called, "early" or "young transitioner" and the second type "older" or "late transitioner" within the transsexual communities. However, the range of age at transition of the two types overlap and this nomenclature may thus be misleading, especially for a "late transitioner" who transitions "early". It is important to remember that the key difference between the two is that the first type is exclusively, or primarily, "homosexual" with regard to natal sex and gender atypical in natural behavior and manner, making it difficult to fit in as their natal sex, while the second type is defined by their atypical sexuality, being aroused by the thought of being or becoming the opposite sex. Think: Laverne Cox vs. Caitlyn (nee Bruce) Jenner.

4 TRANSGENDER

The media and the press often talk as though "transgender" = "transsexual". That is to say, that there is an assumption that those who identify as transgender are all socially transitioning from one social sex to the other, prescribed cross-sex hormones, and either have or would strongly consider, if affordable, surgical interventions. Nothing could be further from the truth, as the vast, in fact, a super-majority, of such self-identified transgender people have not, nor do they wish to, permanently socially transition, nor are they gender dysphoric.

We also need to know how many people fall into each category, as it directly effects policy and politics, from school bathroom use to potential medical transition services demand in the military.

In a 2016 paper exploring this very issue, spelling it out in the title, *"Prevalence of Transgender Depends on the "Case" Definition"*, paraphrasing their results,

"27 studies provided necessary data for a meta-analysis to evaluate the epidemiology of transgender and examine how various definitions of transgender affect prevalence estimates and to compare findings across studies that used different methodologies, in different countries, and over different periods. Overall estimates per 100,000 population were 9.2 for surgical or hormonal gender affirmation therapy and 6.8 for transgender-related diagnoses. Of studies assessing self-reported transgender identity, the estimate was 871; however, this result was influenced by a single outlier study. After removal of that study, the estimate changed to 355."

These numbers tally very well with those from another study using US Census and Social Security data in which name and sex were changed in various US states. In that study no state had more than ~10 per hundred thousand. That means that there are only ~100,000 transsexuals in the United States. And since we know that only about 20% of them are "early transitioners", there are only ~20,000 transsexuals who were transsexual children (i.e. not autogynephilic). Note that this study was not included in the meta-analysis conducted by Collins, et al.

These numbers also tally with the several order of magnitude larger estimates of those who self-identify as "transgender".

One of the most enlightening results of the Collins study was that though there was a slight increase in the number of gender dysphoric cases in a given clinic over time, there was no increase in prevalence over all. That is to say, there is no "epidemic" of gender dysphoria.

The word "transgender" was originally coined and used by Dr. Virginia Prince, a full time autogynephilic cross-dresser, in the early '70s, to denote those like her/him as opposed to "transsexuals" who took hormones and had "sex change" surgery and also opposed to secretive "transvestites" who only occasionally cross-dressed, usually in private. The term was meant to be exclusive of any other group, like drag artists or gender atypical gays or lesbians, AND transsexuals.

But...

In the early '90s, Beth Elliott, using her nom de plume Mustang Sally, wrote an essay entitled, "The Incredible Shrinking Identity" in which she decried the social effects of subsuming transsexual people into the larger umbrella of "transgender", which with each passing year seemed to be growing at its margins to include more and more people who just a few years before, would never have been considered to be in the same grouping. Of course, she was mostly talking about grouped with, under an inclusive umbrella term, secretive cross-dressers, "transvestites", autogynephilic men, who as we know, are in fact in the same etiological taxon as autogynephilic MTF transsexuals. In the '90s, it was possible to ignore this complaint as being specious on the social level, given already rampant socially unwanted and scientifically unwarranted lumping of autogynephilic and exclusively androphilic MTF transwomen (transkids).

But what started as merely political embarrassement (for AGP transwomen) has now become a serious scientific and civil rights issue as the term "transgender" has now been stretched to the point where it has little meaning as to actual sexual, social, or gendered behavior. It is no longer enough for scientists to differentiate between autogynephilic/late onset vs. androphilic/early onset MTF transwomen... nor even between autoandrophilic vs. androphilic FtM transmen... now we must differentiate between an ever growing host of self-defined "other" gender categories and underlying behaviors, This identities that are lumped under "transgender" to the point of making the term meaningless to sexologists and social scientists alike. Worse, for transsexual children and teens, being grouped together with non-gender-atypical / non-gender-dysphoric individuals distorts and even obscures their unique nature and needs.

Flashback, 1980: Hanging out in the L.A. transsexual community, as it gained a political self-awareness, was a teenager; let's call her "Lee". Lee would tell anyone who asked that she was "transsexual"... yet caused great confusion to all who met her. She was natal female, short even for a woman, pleasantly plump, and decidedly feminine in both appearance and manner. She was in no sense gender atypical. And during the time that I knew her, over 18 months, she never made any attempt to present as a man, nor even as butch. She was always on the femmy side of androgynous to the point of being decidedly "cute" as she hung out, mostly with younger MTF transwomen whom she seemed to admire. Had she been hanging out in this same manner in the gay male scene, they would have likely labeled her a "Fag Hag". The transsexual community, while leery of non-trans males who would have acted this way, affectionately accepted Lee's non-threatening presence, while secretly rolling their eyes when she declared that she was "FtM".

Thinking back on Lee, I'm fairly certain that she never transitioned and I'm willing to place fairly high odds that she married and had kids, probably now has grandchildren, none of which have any idea that she once hung out in the trans-scene. At the time, we had no label for her. Today, on the internet, the FtM transsexual community does have a label that would have applied, "tucute", as in "Too Cute" to be transsexual. If you visit the FtM pages on Tumbler, you are sure to run into quite a few... and will also note that they in turn, grumble about the negative feedback they get from those they call "Truscum" ("true" masculine gynephilic FtM transsexuals) for not accepting that they too are just as "trans", even if they are in no sense gender atypical nor gender dysphoric.

Recent Events: Around 2015, via her facebook page, a very socially liberal, rather prominent (and wealthy) venture capitalist in my professional circle proudly announced that her teenaged child was "transgender". I've been living "mostly stealth" in that most of my professional contacts do not know of my medical history (yes, I "pass"). But in a move to be supportive and perhaps even help her with the emotional issues that almost always come with a child's transition I came out to her. BAD MOVE! Nope, upon learning more about her child, it became very clear that her daughter had always been very gender typical as a girl, was not the least bit gender dysphoric, and had no intention of legally, socially, nor medically transitioning. No, she just wanted to be recognized as "transgender" and have everyone around her use gender neutral pronouns (cause ~~she is~~ *they are* so special, ~~she~~ *they* deserves it).

There is another couple names for this behavior, "TransTrender" and "TrendsGender", as in it is now "trendy" to say that one is transgender, or "non-binary", in the right circles.   Back in my college years, hanging around Stanford University, I would often hear complaints from actual gynephilic women, real lesbians, about the phenomena of primarily androphilic women taking social positions as "Political Lesbians" and "Lesbians Until Graduation".   The "transgender" community now has the same phenomena. It seems to have become "cool" in some comfortably well off, very socially liberal teenaged and young adult circles to be associated with the LGB and now T community, as though being associated with a marginalized group made up for their obvious social privilege.

One could well imagine the growing resentment felt by those of us who have experienced familial rejection, social disapprobation, economic deprivation, and psychic pain from a lifetime of gender atypicality and dysphoria towards those who misappropriate an identity from the protective cocoon of indulgent family, liberal universities, and the anonymity of the internet.

As one young transman put it,

> *"Dysphoria is the defining factor of a transgender person. It's why they want to TRANSition. It's why they're called TRANS in the first place, fuckwits. It doesn't have to be crippling "I hate my body ugh I can't look at myself naked" (And I do know some trans people whose dysphoria is that bad). On a 10 is an "I can't see myself naked" to 1 is a "I don't feel right in this body", I'm probably a 5-7. I can see myself naked but it just doesn't feel right. Specially with my*

chest. That's dysphoria. Not "omg I don't want to be human I want to be a rabbit/sunflower/magical girl" or whatever these tucutes are on I don't even know. ...

The more I look at it, the more I see tucutes acting like being transgender is a cute little accessory they can put on. You're comfy with your body but you like girls even if you're a girl yourself? Congratulations, you could be a lesbian. You like boys but you're a boy? Good on you, you might be a homosexual man. You like the opposite gender? That makes you a terrible hetero person and that's bad because all hetero people are transphobic and evil. Be trans instead. That's cooler.

Except... it's not.

It's not cool to be trans. It's not cool to wake up and see these parts of you that you feel so uncomfortable with having that you would wish cancer on yourself just to have them taken away. It's not cool to have to struggle with the longing to tell your parents that you're not the right gender because you want to trust them and want to open up to them but you're afraid it'll just add to the laundry list of things you've already disappointed them with. It's not cool to have known you were one thing from birth but everyone else and your own body telling you you're not and that you were supposed to be a certain way because that's what you looked like from the outside.

It's not cool to be trans.

If I had a choice, if being trans WAS a choice I would choose to be cis."

If these issues had stayed on the pages of tumbler and facebook, it wouldn't be a problem for science or those seeking better civil rights for transitioning transfolk. It wouldn't be a problem for parents of transsexual children and teens. It wouldn't be a problem for actual transsexual youth. But it hasn't.

Consider a recent paper published in the Journal of Youth and Adolescence in which the authors very laudably explore the issues of safety and bathroom access for "transgender" youth. Ah... you are probably anticipating some of the problems that this might entail and you would be right. But let's explore each of them carefully.

They found that at one high school that 9% of the teenagers "identified" as "trans"!!!

The authors cite the now popular William's estimate of 0.7% of the population in the US as "transgendered". The problem with that study is that is the number who **identify** as "transgendered" because William's did not apply any operational definition beyond asking if they were "transgendered". Yet we know that only 0.03% of the U.S. population has actually socially transitioned, according to US Census study that cross-correlated with name/sex status changes to Social Security cards (arguably the absolute best estimate we will ever get to the number of individuals who actually transitioned). This means that less than 5% of those who *identify* as "transgender" ever transition. Thus, by definition, more than 95% of those who *identify* as "transgender" never transition, that in fact, they aren't at all gender dysphoric. So who are they?

Most of them are heterosexual men who occasionally cross-dress in private, classic autogynephilic transvestites, but among teens and young adults who publically declare that they are "trans"? Most of them are young women who for various reasons want to sit at what they perceive to be the 'cool kids lunch table', as claiming to be "trans" or "non-binary" gives them a feeling of being special.

There is political concern about these non-gender-dysphoric teens, falsely claiming to be "trans" in that as they grow up, they 're-identify' as typical young women and thus are falsely labeled "detransitioners" and weaponized by transphobic propagandists whose goal is to outlaw medical services for transsexual teens.

Already, their large numbers and publically claiming to be "trans" has caused great distress to many parents who have in turn invented their own term to explain these young women, "Rapid Onset Gender Dysphoria" (ROGD). Problem is, they aren't actually gender dysphoric, but the label is used as though they are seeking medical interventions, when they, by and large, as we saw above, are not.

Because of this confusion, many parents of transsexual teens, in deep denial, turn to this new explanation and insist that their child has ROGD and are not transsexual.

Discovering that one's child is gender dysphoric, for whatever reason, evokes parental distress. How can it not? The specter of one's child going through pain is bad enough. But to "lose" the child that one thought one had, as though they were dying, and yet that child isn't dying but may metamorphose into another, a stranger, a changeling?

Even for parents who believe that they are liberal, tolerant, accepting of LGBT people, that "loss" is still real.

These parents grieve for the child that they thought they had. The grief is real. It hurts. Even as they love their gender dysphoric child, they still grieve.

Which brings us to how grief is experienced and expressed. Although often questioned, the Kübler-Ross model is still generally useful if we disregard the notion that one goes through it in a linear progression. Instead, the "stages" can be experienced in a wicked jumble. They are denial, anger, bargaining, sadness, and (hopefully), acceptance.

Parents of gender dysphoric children will exhibit all of these emotions and expressions. But now, with the internet to allow parents to very quickly find each other, these personal expressions can take on social expressions.

Unlike the actual death of a child, a child who is gender dysphoric and wanting to socially transition is still standing there, day in, day out, so the grieving stage of denial has no easy check, their child could be mistaken, it could all be just a phase, a fad, a social contagion. It could be this false malady that other parents are all talking about, Rapid Onset Gender Dysphoria... and it should be treatable! It will all be OK. My child won't grow up to be one of *those people.*

But the child still stands there and still insists that they feel this awful disconnect between their body, their social expectations, their sexuality, and what they dare to dream for their future selves. The parents feel frustrated, and the next stage of grieving comes to play, anger. Anger at the child, but that isn't the real problem they say to themselves, it must be someone else's fault. It must be all of that stuff on the internet. It must be all of that *Transgender Ideology* that has gotten into their innocent heads, causing Rapid Onset Gender Dysphoria. *Those People* are to blame. And when *those people* won't take responsibility for hurting their child, well, it's time they were castigated for it on the internet!

But sometimes, the parents need to bargain. Oh… couldn't we find a therapist to fix my child. Shouldn't there be some sort of therapy allowed for my child? Why is conversion therapy no longer legal? Surely I'm allowed to determine what is best for my child?

Then the sadness strikes and they look to the internet to find advice on how to cope with a transgender child, how to deal with a transgender child. Fruitlessly searching for those magic words that will make the pain go away.

And maybe, just maybe, they will finally reach acceptance and learn to celebrate the child that they have, rather than continue to grieve the loss of the child they thought they had.

Parents in online fora are grasping at the concept of ROGD as they work their way through their grieving for their gender dysphoric child. It is not their child's etiology. But as reason for castigating transfolk and an imaged harmful "transgender ideology" it serves the purposes of a number of transphobic constituencies to take advantage of grieving parents.

5 DESISTING AND PERSISTING

For physicians and other health care providers, an over-riding concern is to "do no harm". One of the fears for such care providers is that of starting a course of treatment intended to treat a condition, only to discover that they misdiagnosed the patient and gave a treatment that not only was unneeded, but potentially harmful.

In the case of trankids, both MTF and FtM, the sooner one can begin hormonal & surgical treatment and social support interventions to allow them to successfully transition into the appropriate gender/sex role so as to take advantage of the normal adolescent physical and social maturation process alongside their peers, the better the long term outcome.

But, as the studies shows, not all gender atypical children will be gender dysphoric, and not all children believed to be gender dysphoric will persist as such into their teen years. Thus, studies were conducted in the hope of finding differences between persistors and desistors, so that clinical treatment decisions can be made as early as possible. The earlier one can separate the two, the earlier one can begin to treat the transkids, while letting non-transsexual teens grow up naturally, without potentially harmful iatrogenic trauma.

Starting with Green's studies at UCLA in the late 1960's, where they had gathered a group of fifty obviously gender atypical boys who they thought were all transsexual, only one of them later transitioned. Instead, the majority came out later as gay or bisexual men. Thus was born the belief that most "transkids" desist being so. Later studies, tightening their selection criteria, showed number like 80% desisted. Yet later studies showed lower numbers like ~50%. But as we shall see, their criteria were still too loose.

Because healthcare providers in the past have not been able to accurately predict which gender atypical / dysphoric children will persist, a number of practitioners have begun recommending and using a puberty blocking protocol, under a harm reduction model in which the persistors are protected from the harmful effects of their endogenous hormones, while refraining from iatrogenic injury from exogenous cross-sex hormones in those who will desist from their earlier gender dysphoria. The current recommendation is that such puberty blockers be used until the individual is 16 or even 18 years old, at which time, if he/she is still a persistor, they may be switched to cross-sex hormones, while the desistors may terminate the puberty blocking protocol at any time. (There is a built in bias for desistors and against persistors in that desistors can begin a preferred hormonal protocol, simply by stopping the puberty blockers, but persistors must wait and "prove" to healthcare workers that they are ready.)

The problem with this protocol is twofold: First delaying puberty for too long reduces the eventual strength of the bones in adulthood. This may not be immediately harmful, but those children will someday be older adults, whose bones will be more prone to breaks. Second, for MTF transkids, delaying puberty means that they will continue to grow taller, potentially reducing their ability to pass successfully as female. This effect may however be welcomed by the FtM transkids, but their desisting female peers may not feel the same.

Another problem with this protocol is that it is very expensive, far more expensive than cross-sex Hormone Replacement Therapy (HRT). For those who live in countries who do not have a generous state provided health plan, this may be a deal breaker.

So, for health care providers and parents alike, it may be better if they can accurately predict who will desist and who will persist. Getting this data is the object the Steensma study. The Steensma study is short on statistics, but what they do have is remarkable:

	Total group (N = 53)	Persisters (N = 29)	Desisters (N = 24)
Natal sex			
% (N) Boys	56.6 (30)	58.6 (17)	54.2 (13)
% (N) Girls	43.4 (23)	41.4 (12)	45.8 (11)
Age at childhood assessment			
M (SD)	9.41 (1.46)*	9.92 (1.26)	8.81 (1.47)
Age at follow-up			
M (SD)	16.11 (1.70)	16.14 (1.84)	16.07 (1.54)

* Significant difference observed between persisters and desisters in age at childhood assessment ($t(51) = 2.968$, $p < .05$), Cohens d = 0.81

The most important data is that there is a difference between the ages of childhood assessment, the age at which their parents brought them to a clinic for evaluation. (The difference being on average a little over a year, or over 10% of their age, and a very large effect size of d = 0.81)

But, the study makes it very clear that there was very little difference between the two groups in their early childhood gender atypicality. So why is there this difference? Why would the parents of persistors wait longer than those of desistors?

Because they don't! It wasn't that parents of persistors waited longer, it was that many desistors, desisted at an earlier age, such that their parents never brought their children in for assessement in the first place! As they get older, fewer and fewer parents of desistors would bring in their children. But, the persistors would continue to be brought in at later and later ages. Indeed, the authors specifically stated that from the interviews, the desistors clearly articulated that from age 10 to 13 were critical for their change in gender dysphoric feelings. While, for persistors, that same age only confirmed and strengthened their feelings. Thus, both interview report and the statistics agree that something special seems to be happening starting at around the age of ten or even a little younger.

"Starting around the age of 10, and for the subsequent years, the persisters indicated that their crossgender preferences and behaviour and their gender identity remained stable, but that their dysphoric feelings

intensified. The intensification of gender dysphoria was attributed to three factors; (1) Certain changes in their social environment, (2) The anticipation of and/or actual physical changes during puberty, (3) The first experiences of falling in love and discovering their sexual orientation."

The authors, in focusing on what the teenagers said were influential, may have missed a critical factor. What's so special about the age of ten? This is well before puberty. The authors focused on changing social factors, but could it be that biology is the important factor? McClintock and Herdt point out that sexual attraction is first noted well before our classic definition of puberty, that of the maturation of the gonads and subsequent increase in testosterone, estrogen and progesterone. Instead, other hormones start earlier, typically around ten years old. And this is the age at which one's sexuality begins to be recognizable.

With regard to sexual attraction, all persisters reported feeling exclusively attracted to persons of the same natal sex, which confirmed their gender identity as they viewed this attraction as a heterosexual attraction. They did not consider themselves homosexual or lesbian.

For the desisting boys, some came to recognize that they were gay or bisexual, essentially confirming the results of many other studies which have shown that gender atypicality in boys is highly correlated with homosexuality. However, a number of the boys self-identified as heterosexual, even though they also recognized some same sex attraction (being in fact, bisexual).

For the girls, all of the desistors had become aware of the fact that they were heterosexually attracted to boys and wanted to be sexually attractive to boys. Thus, they were the classic tomboys who grow up to be straight women. But the persisting girls were all attracted to girls.

Thus, this study showed that the key difference between persistors and desistors among female bodied gender atypical / dysphoric individuals was sexual orientation, but among male bodied, it was not as clear cut, desisting and persisting boys both included androphilic sexual orientations. However, what is clear is that persisting boys are all clearly unambiguously androphilic (attracted to men).

Persistors will demonstrate same sex attraction, while desistors may or may not. Thus opposite sex attraction is a key exclusionary sign for persistors.

Another point can be clearly found in the Steensma study is that the developmental process, whatever it is for desistors, is finished by age 14 at the latest. If a gender atypical 14 year old is still gender dysphoric and wishes to begin hormones and transition, we can be reasonably certain that he or she will not change his/her mind later. Thus, based on the evidence, we can safely begin such interventions. The sooner the better.

A more recent study from the University of Washington went into much deeper detail into the level of gender dysphoria, gender identification, and personality, found,

"Children from our longitudinal cohort who would later transition were highly similar to transgender children

(children who had already socially transitioned) and to control children of the gender to which they would eventually transition. Gender-nonconforming children who would not go on to transition were different from these groups. These results suggest that (a) social transitions may be predictable from gender identification and preferences and (b) gender identification and preferences may not meaningfully differ before and after social transitions."

What this basically demonstrates is that transsexual children really are just that. That one CAN tell the difference between persistors and desistors and that social transition follows gender identity. Desistors didn't chose to socially transition. In essence, persistors were like gender typical children of the opposite sex in nearly every way and took to social transition like ducks to water. This demonstrates that social transition for children is just as effective as the notorious "real life test" for adults.

From the evidence, we draw the conclusion that for obviously gender atypical / dysphoric teens, waiting until one is 16 or 18 years old to end puberty blocking protocols and beginning HRT is unwarranted and ill-advised. Instead the evidence points to the age of 14 as the latest that HRT may safely be begun with little risk of iatrogenic injury to desistors. Indeed, the evidence suggests that carefully evaluated, many of the desistors may be excluded by age ten to twelve. Another point to come of these studies is that anatomic dysphoria (discomfort with genitalia, etc.) and successful social transition are correlated with persistence. Thus, if delaying puberty is chosen, it should not be continued past the 14th birthday, and given proper screening, may be ended earlier, to switch to HRT. For both cost and health reasons, it may be best to start on HRT for those who clearly fit the profile of a transsexual, post social transition, who request and understand the consequences of HRT, as soon as would be indicated for their gender of choice. That is to say, that for MTF's, HRT should begin at age 12, and for FtM, at around age 14, mimicking the natural maturational process for each target sex.

6 TRANSSEXUAL CHILDREN

Just as children come in all shapes and sizes, personalities and temperaments, children also show a range of gender expression. To say that a given behavior is masculine or feminine is to say that males or females are more or less likely to behave in such a manner. But no one individual is "purely" masculine or feminine. However, if you know a transkid, you will also know that they are different. Transkids are very obviously gender atypical, from the way they talk, move, sit, play, etc.

Transkids who were born male are like little girls, often interested in playing with other little girls, playing girl games, dressing up, into stories and images of princesses, taking the role of "mommy", perhaps interested in baby dolls or Barby dolls. They walk like girls. They have a distinctly feminine speech pattern, they sound like girls. They typically hate playing boy games, avoid rough and tumble play, and may "throw like girls" when required to play ballgames. As teens, they are interested in fashion, make-up, and handsome BOYS! Many (but not all), love to be around babies and younger children, seeking out babysitting or other childcare activities.

Transkids who were born female are like little boys, often interested in playing with other little boys, playing boy games, into stories and images of masculine heroes (or villains), love loud, boisterous rough and tumble games. They typically hate playing girl games, especially "house" or other make-believe games. They may HATE having to dress up in feminine clothes. As teens, they are interested in sports, athletics, skate-boards, fast cars or motorcycles, and pretty GIRLS!

Underneath the outward behavioral difference, which, while always present, there is an additional personal repugnance for one's own sexed body, which if not directly observable, may be discerned by careful observation. For example, a transkid may be very reluctant to discuss or allow others to observe their genitals and/or secondary sexual characteristics, even parents or healthcare providers. This reluctance is not simple modesty, but deep-seated revulsion. This repugnance only grows with the passing years, especially during puberty.

In a sense, if you ignore their original birth sex, they would have been very gender typical had they been seen as the opposite sex from the beginning. However, if they are forced to conform to gender norms of their birth sex, they become withdrawn, sad, and prone to emotional outbursts. They may have difficulty with school, unable to focus on tasks.

Special problems before transition

If your child is enrolled in a single sex school, classes, or youth groups, your child will be under greater scrutiny. Gender atypical children are under far greater pressure to conform to gender norms in single sex settings, which may evidence itself from social isolation, verbal disapproval, to physical bullying. They are also more stressed and uncomfortable in such situations, feeling out-of-place and lonely, a fish out of water. Do not require your child to be in such environments. They will not help your child to learn to "fit in better"... and will only increase your child's awareness of their atypicality, in a negatively valued manner.

Many gender dysphoric children feel extremely uncomfortable wearing clothing that is especially iconic of their birth sex, especially if that clothing exposes or reveals their body. For example, MTF transkids feel "exposed" if they are required to wear a boy's bathing suit, exposing their upper body, as they feel that they are exposing what girls in our culture would never expose. Similarly, FtM transkids feel humiliated at being required to wear feminine dresses and accessories, in exactly the same manner as would a typical boy who was forced to wear such clothing. Clothing that is specifically designed for anatomic reasons (e.g. undergarments) may be a special source of shame and humiliation.

One of the most anxiety provoking situations for young gender dysphoric children or teens is using a public restroom, especially if there are other children or adults present. They may avoid it as long as possible, giving rise to 'accidents', often just in sight of home. Do not chastise your child for this. (Consider, would you be comfortable going into the restroom of the other sex? With members of that sex also present? REALLY?) Forcing the child to use a public restroom may induce lifelong "shy bladder" or "shy bowel" syndrome, not just temporary distress. A short-term problem is the increased risk of bladder infections and painful constipation. You may need to plan trips to avoid the need for public restroom visits.

Similarly, only amplified, the requirement for those in middle or high school to change and shower in a public locker room is extremely distressing. Many transkids refuse to change or shower in such a situation. Or, if they do, they go to great lengths to achieve what privacy they can. This reticence is two-fold: on one hand is being exposed to others who they experience as being the "opposite gender" to their own (never mind any biological sex similarities), the other is that of extreme repugnance and embarrassment over their own sexed body, which they feel to have been a "birth defect", and not truly representative of their proper gender. Refusal to change or shower in front of others will often result in official reprimand from gym instructors, who are unlikely to understand and/or sympathize with transyouth.

Sometimes, very little things may be the "final straw" for a youngster, causing upset greater than what the provocation would normally warrant. For example, yet *another* long day spent in school, where the child is required to "line-up" by sex before entering the class, told to pair up by sex for classroom assignments, and they are required to take a role in a class skit or folk dance that is congruent with their natal sex, but not their internal sense of self. Finally, they do something good, and the teacher or other adult says, "Good boy" or "Good girl" as the case may be... Such a situation may cause deep upset and resentful outbursts, experiencing the complement as further pressure to conform to gender norms that are not natural to them, or even as deliberate veiled insults, leaving adults bewildered, with a belief that the child is deeply emotionally disturbed. (Sound familiar? How would you feel in the same situation, being who you are?)

7 ADVOCATING FOR YOUR CHILD

As you step forward to help your child navigate the difficult job of growing up "different", you *will* be second guessed by others, possibly by other family members, by insensitive neighbors and fellow church congregants, by ignorant school officials, and especially by hateful strangers. You may be told that you shouldn't "encourage" your child to be "that way". Some may even accuse you of forcing your children to be transgender. You may find that other parents refuse to allow your child to socialize with theirs. You may also find others who will be dripping with false understanding and sympathy, saying how unfortunate you are to have "such a child". Increasingly, other parents of transsexual kids who are in serious denial or otherwise antipathetic to their children's needs are going online and on social media spreading transphobic propaganda targeting accepting parents with misinformation and shaming tactics. None of this is "fair"; but life is seldom "fair".

Just as your child didn't "choose" to be gender atypical. You didn't either. You are neither a victim nor a villain. You are simply a parent trying to be a good one. Your child is neither a victim nor a villain.

S/he is simply a kid who is different from most, but still worthy of love and understanding, still worthy of being celebrated for being themselves, not just "tolerated", or even just "accepted", but truly *celebrated*, just as any other child.

Though you may not have chosen this role, you need to be an advocate for your child. You must stand up, be counted, and face down those who would treat your child and family as lesser than other children and families.

By all means, be an advocate for your child... but don't expose your child to the media. Someday, your child may regret having his or her story in the press, and even worse, photos or video on YouTube, etc. Most adults who were transkids prefer to live quiet, private lives. Don't preclude that as an option.

As discussed above, using public restrooms before transition may be very distressing for your child. You may wish to discuss the issue at your child's school to find suitable alternatives. Before transition, excusing the child to visit the restroom during regular class time so as to be alone, or to visit the restroom at the nurses office are two possible solutions. After transition, this should not be an issue, as long as the restroom has stalls with doors for privacy, since they will be using the restroom congruent with their preferred gender. If you live in a locality where even after transition, school or other authorities insist that your child use the facilities based on birth sex, please consider moving to another locality. Also, there is nothing immoral about allowing a post-transition child to be stealth and simply not informing said authorities of your child's transsexual status. (When I enrolled in college classes, I "failed" to mention mine.)

We can't wrap our children in a protective cocoon, but chronic bullying is never "OK". You will want to speak up at your child's school if bullying occurs. Take a good look at your child's teacher(s) and school administrators. They too may be a source of subtle bullying, even out-right verbal bullying, or of encouraging their other charges to be bullies by refusing to acknowledge or interfere with such behavior. Don't accept any excuses, "sticks'n'stones", etc. Bullying hurts, even if it's only verbal. Research has shown that chronic verbal bullying or social isolation causes lifelong negative health consequences, both physical and emotional. Verbal bullying can and often does escalate to physical violence directed at gender atypical youth.

Don't overlook your trans' child's siblings. They too may be bullied or targeted for social ostracism because of their relationship to their gender atypical sibling. Such siblings may even turn to bullying or ostracizing their own transkid sibling as a way of winning social approval. Speak up! Do something. If this continues too long, it may permanently damage the sibling relationship, and even your relationship with your trans' child, who will, rightly, look to you as being responsible. Sometimes, siblings can be a great help in protecting a kid from bullying, usually an older brother of a feminine MTF transkid; but it isn't really their job. It's yours.

Don't let your child drop out of school to avoid bullying; Too many transkids drop out and never return. If necessary, transfer your child to a new school. Some parents may opt for homeschooling. If you chose this option, be sure that your child has opportunities to socialize with supportive peers.

Also, don't let the fear of bullying stop you from helping your child transition or allowing other natural gender expression. Bullying is usually far worse before transition, and decreases after, due to being more gender congruent. Further, keeping a child from transitioning or insisting that they be less gender atypical because one fears that they will be bullied is a not so subtle form of "blaming the victim", telling that child that they wouldn't be bullied if they weren't a transkid, that the bullying is their fault. Remember, transkids did not choose to be such, and it is nearly impossible for a child to monitor one's natural gendered mannerisms for more than a few minutes at a time.

You may also need to look at your own home life. Too often, transkids come from homes where even loving parents, close relatives, or neighbors unwittingly create a hostile home life for their transsexual child:

-Often one or more relatives will attempt to "toughen up" an MTF transkid, "be a man!" by insisting on teaching that child how to box or play football; or they may push an FtM transkid to "be more feminine" around company by insisting that child wear that special dress that grandma bought for them.

-Sometimes family will attempt to "manage" a child's gender atypicality by setting time schedules and places when&where it is "ok" to be atypical, but insist on gender typical behavior and attire at other times&places, as though a child can control their gender expression at will.

-It is common for relatives or neighbors to go overboard in trying to "correct" a child's gender atypicality by giving gifts that are overly stereotypical of a child's natal sex (e.g. a football helmet to a child that would rather take ballet, or a Barby Doll™ or make-up to a child who would rather play football). You can trust that the child will get the hint that they aren't acceptable as they are, and will feel very bad because they know that they should express gratitude for the gift, but feel only shame and resentment instead.

-A relative or neighbor may verbally tease, chastise, or even bully a transkid over their gender atypical appearance, mannerisms, or interests in an attempt to change them (e.g. a father grabs his MTF child's growing long hair, yanking the head back angrily, and yells *"What's next?! Are you going to wear barrettes in your hair now?!"* or a neighbor finds that child helping her daughter hem up her skirts yells scornfully, *"Don't you know how boys are supposed to act?"*). That relative or neighbor may feel that this will help your child "fit in better". Trust me, it won't! These subtle and not so subtle messages to your transkid will only cause them to experience shame and true low self-esteem.

-A parent or sibling may recognize the tell-tale signs that a transkid has a crush on another child or teen of the same natal sex, but instead of honoring that child's natural sexuality, push that child toward "dating" the opposite natal sex, pretending that that child's peer friends (e.g. an MTF teen's female friends / and FtM's male friends) are his/her romantic partners. This may cause deep embarrassment (e.g. the father of an MTF teen gently punch's his child's shoulder and makes a lewd remark about that child's best, female, friend, *"You lucky dog!"* or the mother of an FtM teen wants to talk about putting her "daughter" on birth control, now that "she" is "dating boys").

Similarly, there have been historically accepted, but totally erroneous beliefs, among a minority of child development "experts" and psychotherapists, that an overly strong emotional bond between the child and their opposite sex parent, or allowing gender atypical children participation in, expressing interest in, or even just being exposed to, gender atypical activities or hobbies leads to gender dysphoria and/or homosexuality. This has led to an emotionally abusive therapy by some child therapists, encouraging opposite sex parents to reduce their involvement in the child, while encouraging the same-sex-parent to become more involved, especially in stereotypical gender typical activities, to punish (up to and including corporal punishment) gender atypical behavior and reward gender typical behavior, as a means of precluding a young child from becoming a transsexual or gay adult. Following or allowing such a course will more likely lead to resentful withdrawal and long-term damage to the parent/child relationships. **Both** parents should endeavor to love, bond with, and accept their children as they are.

I can attest from personal experience, that nothing could be further from the truth. I was and remain very close to my father, while my mother was and remains cold and distant; and both consistently disapproved of my gender atypicality, encouraging my gender neutral hobbies and regularly attempting to encourage, one may say requiring, stereotypically gender typical ones, which were universally rebuffed by me, from an early age.

Another, less recognized, form of hostile home environment occurs after a transkid teen comes out as such, when one or both parents are in denial of their child's deep and growing discomfort about the physical changes occurring during puberty and adolescence. For a transkid, these changes, though welcomed in normal children, are experienced as deeply disturbing. They (we) see them as being like a serious mistake of nature, making them feel ugly and freakish.

Parents in denial, whose own memories of their own teen years do not include such concerns, may dismiss, often in angry terms, their child's distress. This distress is not just temporary. The changes that puberty brings are permanent and will cause problems for transkids when they later transition, entailing greater medical procedures to reverse (electrolysis for beards, mastectomy for breasts, etc.) and problems with appearance that appears "funny", broad shoulders / narrow hips on a woman (MTF), narrow shoulders / broad hips on a man (FtM).

To understand the nature of their distress consider that for an MTF transkid, that she finds the growth of a beard as would a typical teenaged girl, with horror at becoming a circus freak, a bearded lady. Instead of looking forward to her body softening into woman's soft curves, her bones and muscles become daily more alien, uglier. Her lovely high voice suddenly turns harsh and alien. The onset of nocturnal emissions ("wet-dreams") become an especially humiliating reminder of one's wrong embodiment.

For an FtM transkid, his budding breasts would be just as embarrassing as they would for any self-conscious teenaged boy with gynecomastia, something to be ashamed of and hidden. Instead of looking forward to growing taller and stronger, to a deeper, more resonant voice, and a maturing young man's beard, his body gets soft and rounded. The onset of menses ("periods") become an especially humiliating reminder of one's wrong embodiment.

To these transkids, their anguished appeals for medical help is denied by parents who view their child's plight as a silly "phase" that they will soon grow out of... or worse, that they know that their child is distressed, but feel a deep anger and hatred toward transsexual people in general, and vow that they will do everything in their power to keep their child from becoming "one of *those* people". As I quoted above, Dr. Fisk's 1975 advice regarding such a course still holds, "*You will win a few battles, but lose the war.*"

More often than loving parents would care to believe, there are also parents who become emotionally and even physically abusive toward their transkid child or teen. From research, and as personally corroborated from personal discussions with numerous transkids, about one out of three transkids are obliged to leave their home as teenagers due to unaccepting or abusive parents. The alternative for these transkids is suicide, an all too frequent occurrence.

You must step in and advocate for your child, with schools, with neighbors, even with your spouse or other relatives. If you don't, it will only lower your child's expectation that they can count on you to be understanding and supportive.

As hard as it may be to imagine, some parents of transkids do not love and support their child, finding their gender atypicality and sexual orientation to be deeply embarrassing or religiously offensive. Research shows that around one-third of MTF transkids are disowned by, or run away from, their disapproving families as teenagers. These teens often turn to "survival sex" or commercial prostitution to support themselves. FtM transkids also lose the support of their families, ending up on the street. All of these kids are at very high risk of transphobic violence and substance abuse. These kids are very difficult to place in foster care, as typical foster parents are ill-equipped to support a transkid in transition. Group homes can be even worse, as this exposes transkids to yet more bullying, as they typically place transkids in the "wrong" gender group in most parts of the country. Imagine placing an emotionally fragile, feminine, MTF transgirl in an all-boys group home, even required to share a room with a boy who may harbor transphobic/homophobic attitudes. Or imagine placing a masculine, but emotionally struggling, FtM transkid boy in a room with a girl, and then have the staff "keep watch" because of homophobic/transphobic concern that he might attempt to have sex with his straight roommate. (I've seen both of these scenarios for myself, first hand.) If you have room in your home and your heart, please consider taking in a transkid, either formally from your local child protective services or informally from the street if they have already reached the age of majority.

Also consider becoming a Court Appointed Special Advocate for foster youth. There is always a shortage of volunteers, but especially those who know the special needs of transkids. You can make a world of difference!

I've had two official foster children, one of whom I legally adopted. I've also had a number of unofficial (over 18 years of age) 'foster' transkids over the years, some of whom have lived with me for a time. Being such a foster-mom is a very rewarding experience. I've also been a CASA for an FtM transkid in foster care, a similarly rewarding, if challenging, experience.

8 TALKING WITH TRANSKIDS

Nearly every parent of a transkid has known for a long time that their child was "different". That child has known it too. But often, far too often, neither has spoken much about it. If this is you and your child, the time to break the ice will be sometime when you are alone with him/her, at some quiet time, when you both have many hours to devote to the topic. Since your child will have been getting negative messages from society in general about their behavior, you should START the conversation with saying something complementary about their behavior that you know the child is proud of themselves. Further, you should tell them that you love and admire them, for being who they are, ALL of who they are. Without this reassurance, your child will be defensive and unable to be open and honest. If at all possible, affirm some aspect of your child's personality and character that is gender atypical, so that they will know that talking about being a transkid will be an acceptable topic. If, as the topic becomes open, you should feel some angst, reservation, or fear, acknowledge it openly as your own problem, NOT your child's. Trust me, they already know it exists. But it helps a great deal to 'lay one's cards on the table'.

If your child is a transkid, at some point, there will likely be a tearful confession of unhappiness and a sincere plea for your help. Remember, not every gender atypical child is a transkid. Most are simply gay or lesbian. A few may be straight. Only your child can make a determination as to which they are. But, it's your job as a parent to love them either way.

If a transkid seems to be angry, resentful, or disrespectful after he or she confides that she is transsexual, as I often am told by anguished parents or school employees, it is usually because their family or other important people in their lives, have not given the emotional reassurances that they have been *heard, respected,* and are still *loved*. One of the single most important signals that transkids use to determine this is *consistent* use of their new name and pronouns. For example, using the child's preferred name and gender in their known presence, but their old name and gender pronouns when that child is believed to be out of earshot, will very quickly be discovered by that child... as "walls have ears". This signals to the child that individual is only paying lip service, and is in actuality, very actively antipathetic to that child. A blanket refusal to use their preferred name is even more powerful evidence of antipathy. Similarly, trying to offer advice on how to be less gender atypical will signal that they aren't loved, but are instead a source of embarrassment.

The absolute worst thing that a parent or other caregiver can do is to tell that transkid that they need to / should "accept themselves as they are"... that is to say, to deny their gender dysphoria and pretend it doesn't exist. It tells that transkid that their pain is less important to that parent or caregiver than that parent's wish for a "normal" child. This single attitude and message has presaged more future parent-child estrangement than any other.

9 SOCIAL TRANSITION

There is no "right way" to transition. There is no "right age" to transition. Each child and family situation is different. While a therapist may be able to help, there are very, very few who are experts at this. But *you* are THE expert of *your* family. That having been said, it is generally recognized that those who transition early in their teen or pre-teen years are happier and better adjusted, than those who are required to wait until they are in their late teens or early 20's.

Although there have been articles in the media about camps for transgender children, which in general are a good thing, as they allow lonely kids to socialize with others like themselves, don't be fooled into thinking that they are a substitute for full-time transition for your child.

As I told my own father when he offered to pay for "vacations" when I was a teenager, if I agreed to live a boy / man the rest of the time, "*I am NOT a part-time woman!*"

However, your child will need to experiment with temporary "transitions", expeditions if you will, in which they interact with peers and adults who do not know that they are transkids, BEFORE, any permanent social transition is attempted. This is so that your child truly will understand if this is the right direction... and if it is even possible for them to pass as non-transsexual in their new social gender. Most transkids do this, with or without parental support, or even knowledge. They may or may not do so in the company of peers. Since the goal of transition is to improve one's chances in life, if they can't ever pass, or they don't find increased social comfort and personal ease during these experiments, they will need to find another accommodation to their situation.

This potential 'other accommodation' may or may not be a happy one, as the alternative is to live as a very gender atypical gay or lesbian teenager and adult. Contrary to popular portrayals, gender atypical, "femme" individuals are not very well accepted in the gay male community, which values the "straight looking / straight acting" ideal. In fact, they can be downright cruel to such individuals. The lesbian community is a bit more accepting of "butch" individuals, but not always understanding of FtM somatic gender dysphoria. The general population is even less accepting of such gender atypical adults. Further, the mismatch between expectations for social behavior for each gender and the natural gendered behavior of gender atypical transkids grow with each year closer to full adulthood they get. Remember, transkids have to live in the real world. It is not their job in life to be "gender warriors" to change all of society with only their brave example, tilting at windmills.

Transkids typically take to social transition like a duck to water. It is the ultimate "test" of whether a child or teen is, or is not, a transkid.

Nothing else really works to differentiate transkids from those that aren't. However, the final decision is one that can only be made by your child. It is, after all, their life, hopefully a long and happy one, that they are making decisions about.

If you honestly do not believe that your child can or should socially transition in your own household, because of other unaccepting family or community issues, consider other options such as other family members who can and would take your child in, e.g., brothers or sisters, your parents, etc. If those are not available or willing, consider foster parenting through networks of other parents of transkids, or even adult (former) transkids themselves. Given that transkids' options for parenting are limited, this may be an ideal option. Your child will become a valued member of an extended family and you will remain in close contact with your child. (Note, I have been a legal foster parent in two states and can easily be re-licensed. If I could do it, so could they.)

Transition for transkids is usually a happy and magical time, her/his dreams of many years are coming true. You will need to monitor it to keep the situation in hand. But it can also be stressful. "Will grandma still love me?" "Will I have friends?" "Can I still play soccer?" You may also discover that your child will seem to "regress" emotionally, need to be like a toddler, checking back in very often for emotional reassurance and safety. This is quite common and expected. If you and the rest of the family are receptive to this process, it will deepen your relationships.

You and other family members may feel awkward for a while, using a new name and gender. It will get better as you see your child blossom in his or her new social identity.

There are many logistical issues that will need to be addressed: school, medical help, therapy (if needed, most transkids don't), informing other relatives and close family friends, etc. You may consider moving to a new neighborhood and school, if financially practical, to allow your child to be "stealth". (Being "stealth", keeping one's post-transition transsexual status private, is a very common goal of transkids as they mature. After all, if "everyone knows"... they haven't really socially transitioned, just dressed differently.) At the very least, transferring to a new school at some practical distance should be considered.

Your other children need to be considered in creating your trans' child's transition plan. They may need to talk to somebody about their feelings, which can range from anger to fear. Be that somebody. Their lives will also be effected by any relocation or school transfer. They may also be effected by bedroom assignment changes that may be needed. There may also be some confusion and uncertainty over what their sibling's transition means for their own sense of self and expectation of stability in others. They too may mourn the loss of the "brother" or "sister" they thought they had. Listening will go a long ways to alleviate their concerns.

Be aware that transsexuality and homosexuality does "run in families". It's not unheard of to have two or even three children in one family. Dealing with one child may bring another child to the point of being willing to talk about their own issues.

10 AT THE DOCTOR'S OFFICE

It almost goes without saying, but you will want to find a sympathetic physician; far too many transkids have had unpleasant experiences with unsympathetic ones! (e.g. an FtM teenager asks his physician for masculinizing HRT and is prescribed birth control instead, in an attempt to fool him {true story} or an MTF teenager asks her long time pediatrician for feminizing HRT, and hears him stutter for the first and only time in horror and angry hate, "Y-y-ou c-can d-do anything y-you want with y-your life… B-b-but I w-w-won't be part of it!" and "fires" her from his medical practice {another true story – mine}.)

First order of business; Have your child vaccinated against **Human Papilloma Virus (HPV)**! All children, both boys and girls should be vaccinated against all of the common viral threats, but MTF transkids are especially vulnerable to HPV because of their sexuality. It is important that MTF transkids be vaccinated against HPV before they become sexually active as teenagers to avoid the risk of HPV induced anal cancer. Even after sex reassignment surgery, these kids are at increased risk of genital cancer caused by HPV due to the nature of the post-operative tissue exposed. (This is not theoretical for me... I too had genital cancer, which required surgery to remove.) On the flipside, the risk of cervical cancer in FtM transkids is likely lower than for gender typical girls... but HPV also causes oral and urogenital cancers. Vaccinate.

You may feel it would be best to find an expert but, in reality, this isn't necessary. Any good general practitioner, gynecologist, or internal medicine specialist will be up to the task of monitoring your child's hormone replacement therapy (HRT). Be aware that many physicians are overly cautious about HRT for transkids, often delaying beginning treatment unnecessarily, or prescribing an ineffectively low dose, fearing iatrogenic harm. Be assured, that if your child has reached the age of 12 or so, and insists on beginning puberty blockers or HRT, he or she is ready and very unlikely to regret this decision. Don't be talked into delaying puberty blockers or HRT; Consider that not being on blockers or HRT is the same thing as being on HRT, but in the opposite direction! Some of the undesired changes from delaying HRT are permanent and should be avoided at all costs. If your child is ambivalent or uncertain, delaying puberty is the safe bet, but don't let the doctors dictate this.

You may have read that using puberty blockers (e.g. Lupron) has become the standard of care for young transkid teens. However, you should be aware that the reason for this is NOT medical, but political. These docs are afraid to begin actual HRT for two reasons, one is reasonable, the other is not. The first reason is the fear of iatrogenic harm... that is, that if they use HRT to begin a teen's physical "sex change" and that child changes their mind, that they will have accidentally done great harm instead of good. The second, unstated reason, is that our society is still uncomfortable with minors making such changes, period. Sadly, this political reason has backfired in that most people antithetical to HRT are just as antithetical to puberty blockers.

What you should know about puberty blocking is that almost no teen who has been put on puberty blockers decided against HRT later. In other words, if puberty blocking (delaying) is supposed to allow time for those teens to "change their minds", it is a rare event. Thus, while delaying is better than allowing a natural puberty to occur, the evidence is that such delay, especially long delay, is unnecessary, just delaying the inevitable. And it is, in my opinion, just plain cruel, as it keeps a transkid teen in limbo, in between looking like a boy and a girl, looking like a prepubescent child, at a time when one should be developing alongside one's peers, making one's social acceptance more difficult. Further, some desired changes that occur earlier in adolescence, will not happen if HRT is delayed on puberty blockers too long, leaving a transkid with a "funny" appearance. (One continues to grow taller on Lupron, so an MTF trankid may grow taller than average for a girl.)

Consider that the "standard of care" for children with certain Disorders of Sex Development, such as hypogonadism, is to start HRT as soon as their peers enter puberty, in order to improve self-esteem and social acceptance. If this protocol is good for one population, why is it not good for another?

However, if your child is on puberty blockers, I highly recommend vitamin D and calcium supplements to reduce the risk of osteopenia.

For MTF transkids, I strongly recommend using "bio-identical" HRT of estradiol and micronized progesterone in combination with an androgen blocker. Avoid estinyl-estradiol, Premarin, Prempro, or anything with synthetic progestins such as medroxyprogesterone; these products are less effective and possibly carcinogenic and neurotoxic. Given that your child will be on a higher dose than natal women typically are... and for her entire life, it's important not to be taking anything but the best available, especially given that they may actually cost less. It is best to maintain a constant dosage, that is to say, that it is not only not necessary, but actually counterproductive, to "cycle" HRT. Monthly cycling of HRT is sometimes practiced in the mistaken belief that it mimics female menstrual cycles.

If puberty blockers or HRT started young enough, facial hair growth is avoided. If she has had some growth, but is still not fully developed, HRT may reverse some of the growth. A physician can also prescribe eflornithine topical cream (Vaniqa) which combined with HRT may control the facial hair. Otherwise, electrolysis and/or laser treatments may be needed.

For FtM transkids, although not typically known, due to lack of research into the special needs of FtM transkids, consider delaying puberty until age 14 with puberty blockers, in combination with low dose testosterone, then adding Human Growth Hormone to the traditional testosterone treatment from age 14 to 22, so as to allow him to reach average male height and build. Boys typically start their growth spurt later and continue to grow taller in their later teen years. The delayed puberty and then added growth hormone will help duplicate this process. If facial and body hair is lacking and desired, consider using minoxidil, available over the counter as Rogaine, topically on the face and limited body areas to accelerate hair growth. (Caution: minoxidil can lower blood pressure, which should be monitored.)

In any case, working closely with a sympathetic and knowledgeable doctor is both prudent and recommended.

11 THERAPY

Most transkids don't need psychotherapy. There is nothing inherently disordered about gender atypicality. And wanting to fit into society better by transitioning is a healthy and rational decision. But, our present "Standards Of Care" for transsexual persons, designed primarily for autogynephilic MTF adults, requires that a psychologist or psychiatrist diagnose an individual as being gender dysphoric, and not psychotic, before HRT may be prescribed. (Truth be told, "Gender Dysphoria Disorder" is, and always has been, a self-diagnoses, as only the individual can really know.) Additionally, one is required to have a "letter" or two from such authorities before a surgeon will perform sex related procedures (i.e. Sex Reassignment Surgery {SRS}, mammoplasty, etc.).

As a parent, you want to do the right thing. You may not hear this advice anywhere else, but this is extremely important: If your child is a transkid and not an autogynephilic teenaged boy, your child will be far better served if the therapist understands the specific needs of transkids. That means that the therapist must also understand and acknowledge that there are two different and distinct biological / psychological etiologies for gender dysphoric people, that transkids are not the same as late transitioning adults. I strongly recommend interviewing prospective therapists to determine their views on this matter. If he or she is not knowledgeable of, or objects to, this understanding... look elsewhere. ***Seriously, look elsewhere.***

Under no circumstances should you allow your child to be counseled by a gender therapist who believes that all transsexuals have the same underlying condition. The reason that this is ill-advised is that gender therapists who hold this view will be seeing a more numerous population of adult transitioning MTF transsexuals who are autogynephilic. The therapist will naturally apply what helps this population to your child, with very confusing, potentially distressing, and counterproductive results.

In a similar vein, don't allow a therapist to encourage your child to read autobiographies of adult transitioning transsexuals. Their stories are not applicable to transkids and they do not serve as approachable role models.

The single most damaging thing that could happen in a therapeutic setting would be to include your transkid in a support group for older adult transitioning transsexuals. Simply put, their etiology, experiences, motivations, and especially sexuality, are at complete odds with transkids' experiences and needs. Asking youngsters to expose their innermost feelings to others is best done with those like themselves.

First and foremost is that the two types should NEVER be placed in the same therapy or support groups, especially the two MTF types.

Some organizations already have practices which do this as an accidental effect by segregating by age, usually a cut-off from 18 up to 25 and under only in their youth group. The '25 and under only' group can be problematic as this only statistically separates the majority of the AGP transwomen. Due to the relatively greater number of AGP transwomen, a sizable number of under 25 autogynephiles will be included in the youth group with negative consequences for all. On the other hand, although using a lower age cut-off may dramatically limit the number of AGP transwomen joining, for early onset / androphilic type, on-going support groups, requiring the now older than this cut-off requires early onset transwomen to associate with older AGPs will have even greater negative consequences. The only real solution is accurate differential diagnoses and segregation on that basis.

One of the most serious negative consequences of combining the two types of MTF transgender/transsexuals is that of sexual objectification and harassment.

Autogynephiles are also gynandromorphophilic. That is, they experience a specific sexual attraction to transsexual people, especially those who are pre-op, young, and naturally feminine in appearance and behavior, to wit, teen and young adult early transitioning transsexuals in transition. This sexual attraction actually exceeds their attraction to women. Imagine the consequences of encouraging open and explicit discussions of sex and gender experiences in a group of comparatively masculine individuals used to lifelong male privilege while including young, naive, feminine individuals who are their most desirable sexual and romantic potential partners, who do not as a general rule welcome such attention from autogynephiles.

A less obvious, but potentially counterproductive consequence of mixing the two types is that the two types will compare and contrast their own experiences and motivations to negative effect. For the autogynephilic type, they will be confronted with clear evidence that they do not live up to their idealization of "transsexuality" and femininity. Under such circumstances, envy and jealousy often arise, disrupting the goals of therapy. For the early onset type, having been incorrectly informed that they are meeting with their peers, may look upon the, by stark contrast, masculine (in both appearance and behavior) autogynephiles and create a falsely negative and confusing impression of themselves. For both groups, the confusion caused by discussing essentially incompatible histories and goals will disrupt any hoped for process. In fact, anger and resentment on both sides may arise, as one group tries to deny obvious autogynephilic motivations and natural gender typicality, attempt to mimic the other's history of gender atypicality; while the other is required to pretend that their experiences are comparable lest they be seen as less than supportive, potentially invoking angry, spiteful responses. One group will express their grief and anger about having been ill-treated growing up for being naturally gender atypical, but expound on how transition has helped them be better accepted by society, while the other group complains that previously they held positions of respect but they now find that a transphobic society treats them worse for having attempted to live as women, but fail to pass.

Even having separated the two groups, a common problem encountered by both types is that of muddled conflation of the two groups experiences and goals by the ill-informed therapist:

The problems of early onset transsexuals of both sexes are primarily social, not personal; they transition to improve their social status, as gender atypical individuals often experience discrimination and social exclusion. If anything, the most common personal issue is that of grieving, loneliness, and isolation from disapproving family. These are young people who have been obviously gender atypical since birth. This may mean that their family is disapproving and may have even disowned their child. They are not exploring their inner sense of "gender identity", which usually implicitly matched their gender atypical behavior since early childhood. They are living with the consequences of their long history of outward gender atypical presentation and sexual orientation. When they decide to "transition" it is not a big decision or change. It usually involves very little disruption to their lives, save for some potential additional disapproval from family or church; contrarily, most experience a social blossoming.

Because some early onset transsexuals experience familial rejection, they are a very high risk of self-harming behaviors running from self-sabotage, substance abuse, risky sexual behaviors, cutting, to suicidal ideation and attempted suicide. These youths need social support services but in many localities, the fact that they are transsexual works against them as they are often placed in wrong sex segregated group homes or unsupportive foster families. Social workers may have a very poor understanding the needs of gender atypical youth and feel uncomfortable working with them. The caring health worker should be aware of these difficulties and provide educational materials and advocate for their clients.

As with all health issues, prevention is better than cure. Health care providers are in a unique position to offer help to families with gender atypical children and teens understand and support their child before relations deteriorate.

The problems of autogynephilic and autoandrophilic transsexuals on the other hand are primarily personal, not social... at least before transition. Most have very successful social lives, careers, marriages, family relationships. They are exploring their shifting inner sense of "gender identity" as they face the incongruity of their outwardly socially successful integration as one sex with their inner and usually secret desire to be the other sex. They are at war with themselves, as they deal with the guilt and shame, the dissonance of being socially successful as one sex, while always, in their inner sex life, obligatorily the other. When they decide to "transition" it really is a big decision and even bigger life change; most experience severe family and often career disruption, along with a sudden introduction to the social stigma of being notably gender atypical, in both behavior and appearance, in their new nominal gender role, unable to pass.

Gender therapists often conflate the two groups, making the common mistake that autogynephilic transexuals are dealing with their gender atypicality, failing to recognize their autogynephilia while simultaneously mistaking the early onset group as dealing with conflicted inner gender identity. For example, suggesting to a transkid that she perform some female gender affirming act in the privacy of her home will only be met with either confusion or derision, as her issues are social, not personal. Suggesting that a member of one group read the autobiographies of the other is less than helpful, for the same reason that combining the two groups for support is a bad idea.

Similarly, do not allow your transkid child to socialize with older transitioning transsexuals. Instead, help your child to find and maintain friendships with other transkids of similar age. If you have an adult (former) transkid in your social circle, that adult may or may not be a good role model, depending on their own circumstances and history... but if you do find a responsible, mature, and successful adult who transitioned as a teenager who can show by example that your child has a good future, by all means, allow that relationship to flourish.

Finally, be aware of the problems that "tucutes", "TransTrender", "TrendsGender", "Non-Binaries", etc. may cause in youth support groups & therapy. There is a natural antipathy between people who are gender atypical & dysphoric and those that are falsely claiming to be. Quite literally, as these young people fill up the seats at what they falsely believe is the "cool kids lunch table" they leave no room for transsexual teens, calling them "TruScum". There are even calls from these non-gender-dyphoric individuals to label and ban the very term "transsexual" as being "transphobic".

12 COMMON ISSUES AFTER TRANSITION

As a child grows through adolescence into adulthood, he or she feels their way through the world of sexuality and romance, with many a joyful discovery, heartache, and sometimes misstep. What is true for non-transsexual children goes double for transkids. They will need your emotional support and guidance. If you let them, they will open up and you will find a stronger bond with them than ever before. However, there are issues that you as a non-(former)-transkid will not truly understand. But you must try.

A common, but misguided, behavior of family, relatives, and neighbors, of transkids who have transitioned is to attempt to "protect" their child. For example, their recently socially transitioned child will go to the bathroom appropriate for their new social gender, while a parent or sibling "stands guard" outside the stall or bathroom door. This behavior only brings unnecessary attention, leading strangers to wonder just why such a guard is needed. Even worse, some family members or other caregivers (teachers / school administrators) may insist that their charge use the "wrong" restroom, inconsistent with their social gender presentation, on the pretext that their legal / biological sex hasn't been changed. This increases the chances for transphobic discrimination and violence... and undermines that child's sense of self. Or a parent may restrict their child's social circle to only those friends who "know", or attempt to inform or educate their friend's parents, in effect "outing" their child, defeating the purpose of transition. You must refrain from these policies. Further, keep an eye on your child's school policies and practices. Don't let the school sabotage your child's social transition by signaling to other students that something is "different" about your child (e.g. on a school outing, placing your child in the "wrong" hotel/dorm room). Your child must, MUST, *MUST*, be treated and regarded as actually being a member of his/her new social gender/sex.

However, it should be understood that transkids in transition are still deeply embarrassed, humiliatingly so, about their bodies and will still not wish to expose themselves, even to their same gender identity peers, perhaps especially not to such peers. Further, post transition transkids will still avoid taking showers in public as they do not wish to "out" themselves. Thus, special accommodations will be needed for school showers until and unless they have had Sex Reassignment Surgery (SRS for MTF) and breast reduction surgery for FtM.

As parents, we would wish that our teenagers not explore their sexuality too intimately. But, being realistic, this exploration *is* going to happen. However, for transkids, this is especially fraught with danger. If your non-transsexual child were dating, you would be worried about unplanned pregnancy. This is of course, unlikely for transkids, both MTF and FtM, for their own, rather obvious reasons, given that transkids are universally attracted to the opposite gender (of identity). However, there are special dangers, especially for MTF transkids, of being seriously physically harmed, even murdered, by boyfriends who discover their date's pre-operative status accidentally. Be sure to meet and vet any and all of your teen's dates. Let them know that your child is loved and protected. Further, discuss this danger with your teen. Devise strategies for safety: staying in public, double dating, carry a cellphone, having and sticking to a pre-approved itinerary, having appropriate chaperones at parties, no drugs or alcohol, etc.

This may be a good time to also have a discussion about 'safe sex' practices. For MTF transkids, buy and supply condoms to them. It is far better to be safe than sorry. {Special note: These condoms are for your child's boyfriend's use, size accordingly.}

At some point, your teen will want to share their medical history with a romantic partner. This is a personal decision that can only be made by him or her. This is where a budding romance can end rather suddenly and dramatically, with attendant heartache, and possibly with a public outing at school, church, or work. (This is why I personally mostly avoided dating any man I knew in the same profession or firm.)

If your child is already "out" at school or church, this may not be an issue. But another issue may arise. That of other people not approving of your teen's gender presentation, and especially of their sexual orientation. Other adults may interfere with your child's romantic life. (e.g. the parents of a romantic partner may forbid or pressure their child to discontinue the relationship. It happened to me in a big way when I started dating my brother's best friend as a teenager. Major family drama!) You may or may not be in a position to advocate for your child in this situation, but you must always be ready to listen with a sympathetic heart to your child in this matter.

A common behavior of disapproving family and close community members is that of attempting to sabotage a transkid's transition by financial coercion, cutting off financial support for school or dependent minor healthcare, in the hopes of making their life so difficult that they 'repent', detransition and return home. They may also practice "outing" the transkid to their new friends, neighbors, educators, and employers; refuse to use their new name and gender in public, etc. Some family & community members may ostracize a transkid, labeling them as sinful or mentally ill. Do not excuse or normalize such behavior.

13 IN THE HOSPITAL

One day, you may accompany your child to the hospital for sex reassignment or other surgery. While the "official" line is that transkids must wait until they are 18 before SRS or other related surgeries, I know for a fact that is not true. A number of teens have had SRS before 18, most at age 17. But this fact is understandably not publicized by the surgeons or their patients. You should begin to plan for medical expenses as soon as you know / learn that your child is a transkid. Review your healthcare insurance options as not all carriers cover SRS and other procedures.

Insist that your child have either a room to themselves, or with another transkid of the same social gender and sexual orientation. Under no circumstance allow your MTF child to share a room with an adult MTF transitioner. The hospital administration usually has no real clue about the realities of transsexuality and transsexuals, and think that we are all the same. No one would think of asking a young lady to share a hospital room with an older straight man... but that is in effect what is happening in hospitals on a regular basis. Autogynephilic MTF transsexuals are sexually attracted to women, and often, even especially, to young MTF transkids. Further, a fair number of autogynephilic individuals sexualize the very act, the process of changing sex, both in themselves and in others. Due to a lifetime of socialization as men, and only limited experience in their new gender role, these individuals often do not recognize appropriate boundaries. Do not allow your child to be so exposed when they are at their most physically and emotionally vulnerable point in their young lives! (I myself had a very upsetting incident when I had SRS in 1981. In 2009, I accompanied a transkid to that very same hospital, who had a similar experience, 28 years after my own.)

14 A FAMILY OF THEIR OWN

Someday, your child will be an adult, a "former transkid". Life does not stop. Joy and heartache do not stop. Your child will hopefully find a loving husband or wife (as the case may be). They will want children, as transkids make excellent parents. For FtM transmen who are married to young women, the choices for bearing children are rather straight forward. They may choose to use a sperm donor, either a stranger (through a sperm bank), or a close male relative of the same generation (brother or cousin), to allow their wives to bear children. For MTF transsexuals, the choices are much harder. To date, we have not yet found a way for MTF transsexuals to bear their own children. So, as many couples in similar situations, they may choose adoption or surrogacy. Fortunately, our society has become much more understanding and accepting of transsexual women adopting children (it wasn't always so... I believe that I am the very first transsexual to have been a foster/adoptive parent through Child Protective Services in the United States, in two states no less, California 1984 – Oregon 1993). But some states and countries, are not yet so enlightened. It may be necessary for your child and her husband to move to a more enlightened locale. Surrogacy may or may not be too expensive, given your child's future finances, but is legally an easier option.

From my family to yours, you have our best wishes...

15 LIES

Until the advent of ubiquitous social media, the main means of "trashing trannies" was mass media and churches. But now, with social media, parents of transkids are bombarded with conflicting messaging from all sides and can have difficulty knowing which information to trust. Just as in politics, there is now a great deal of "fake news", propaganda, misinformation, half-truths, even outright lies to be found online. Some of it from people whose only interest is to hurt transkids because of religious or socially formed trans- and homophobia. Some of it is from transphobic parents of transkids themselves. There are even websites and discussion fora created by these very same parents bringing together such like-minded folks to create a wave of disinformation, fear, uncertainty, and doubt in others so as to bolster their own decisions to deny their own children the respect, agency, and medical services they so clearly need.

In this chapter I gather such propaganda and explore how it works and why it is wrong. My goal is to help parents recognize when others are trying to manipulate their emotions to effect their decision-making.

With popular celebrities like JK Rowling of Harry Potter fame now spreading much of these lies and disinformation, it is more important than ever to separate what is fact from what is fiction.

If this chapter seems overly long, blame the voluminous amount of such hateful propaganda that has been created and spread.

Quoting Transfolk Out of Context

This is so classic that it needs only to be mentioned in passing.

Bad History

One sure fire propaganda tool is to set out a revisionist history of the treatment of Gender Dysphoria. Those who control the memory of the past, control understanding of the present.

One trick is to lie and say that the term 'gender dysphoria' is new and replaced the older (and presumably more accurate) Gender Identity Disorder for political reasons under pressure from "transgender rights activists". The real history is that "Gender Dysphoria", a medical term coined by Dr. Norman Fisk at Stanford University in the early 1970s, was included in the Stanford Gender Dysphoria Clinic name and was incorporated in the name of the professional organization, Harry Benjamin International Gender Dysphoria Association formed in the late '70s (more recently renamed World Professional Association for Transgender Health). The term was coined in a deliberate choice to normalize access to medical services for autogynephilic clients. Before then, they were typically denied services. Such services were reserved for "true transsexuals", i.e. transkids.

Another trick is to falsely claim that transsexuality was only about adult sexuality and that children were never part of the picture until very recently. They sweep under the rug such books as Green's 1974 *Sexual Identity Conflict in Children and Adults*. Children and teens, transkids, were being seen from the beginning. Teenagers were being seen and very quietly transitioning, either as run-aways, throw-aways, or for the lucky few, living at home with supportive family. Sadly, its also true that some kids were treated abominably in futile efforts to "cure" them (more below). Transkids, then called "primary" or "true" transsexuals, have always been with us, but they (we) were largely invisible, a despised underclass, criminalized by the law, pathologized by psychiatry, problematized by society, church, and family.

"Transgender Ideology"

The moment you read or hear someone use that term, the material that person is going to share is propaganda. Those familiar with the culture war against gay rights and marriage equality will recognize its propaganda equivalent *"Homosexual (or Gay) Agenda"*. Of course that agenda was social and legal equality. *"Transgender Ideology"* is a search for social and legal recognition, and access to medical services, nothing more. Any other claims are just disinformation. Both of these terms are meant to invoke nebulous distrust of the motives and actions of the LGB & T communities.

We also see people making calumnious claims that transgender people are trying to "indoctrinate" kids into being transgender. This is very much in keeping with the old anti-gay equivalent of "recruiting" young people into the "gay lifestyle". Sadly, such false claims are even being made by transphobic gays and lesbians (no group is too small or too oppressed that it can't turn and do the same to an even smaller and weaker group).

However, when you read claims of "Transgender Ideology", there is an ideology that may be at play... *theirs!*

Another loaded term in vogue is "industry", as in "medical industry", "transgender industry" or just "gender industry". The term falsely invokes the concept of a large and uncaring medical industrial complex out to make as much money out of poor hapless kids and their parents, destroying lives, rather than the deeply caring doctors and therapists that actually exist.

Another means of subtly invoking distrust of transfolk is to describe various elements of the quite disparate transgender communities as the "transgender lobby", likening them to powerful business groups that gain disproportionate power through chummy relationships with lawmakers and regulators. This is a classic trick whereby one falsely paints a marginalized group as secretly powerful.

In the same manner, every transperson who speaks out is labeled an 'activist' (often shortened to the acronym, "TRA") with a smug undertone that 'trans rights activist' means a person with a not to be trusted self-serving "agenda".

A very recent and subtle twist is to use the term "transgender movement", as though the existence of transfolk itself was a "movement" or fad, rather than the correct term "transgender RIGHTS movement". Consider that the push for equality under the law for non-white people was not called the "Colored Movement", but the "Civil Rights Movement".

A popular term meant to subtly disempower transkids and transsexual adults is "gender confusion" to replace "gender dysphoria". It implies that transsexuals are just "confused" and likely mentally challenged and should just "look in their pants!". When you see that term, you know that the speaker / author is no friend of transfolk.

I recently saw a man post a whopper of a lie on a website telling parents that childhood gender dysphoria was an early sign of developing schizophrenia!

One clever rhetorical trick is to create a false comparison by showing that their propaganda can't be labeled "transphobic" because true / real 'phobia is when people are physically abused, beaten, tortured, etc. Transpeople aren't being lynched or gay bashed (actually, we are...). But they fail to acknowledge that dehumanizing language sets the stage for that treatment. While working against one's civil, legal, or human rights is just another tool of the bigot. And in the case of transfolk, working to deny access to reasonable and affordable medical care is just as damaging and cruel.

Blaming the Internet and Other Transkids / Adult Transsexuals

A recent meme to question the validity of gender dysphoria in teenagers is the concept of "Rapid Onset Gender Dysphoria" (ROGD) in which being trans is described as a "social contagion". Gee... that's just saying this is a "fad"... and like the old "phase" claim that transkids were discredited with in the past. Of course, there is the problem that it has become trendy to claim a "trans" or "non-binary" identity, but these kids and young adults are NOT gender dysphoric. The existence of these non-gender dysphoric teenagers and young adults falsely claiming a "trans' or "non-binary" identity is easily weaponized to discredit the existence and sincere social and medical needs of transkids, especially as these non-gender-dysphoric teens and young people drop their claim to being "trans" to claim a new identity as "detransitioners". Detransitioning does exist. It is usually found in adult transitioning autogynephilic males who later regret having attempted transition when they find it doesn't actually help them. However, detransitioning is extremely rare in actual gender dysphoric teenaged transkids and former transkids (transsexual adults who were gender dysphoric as children).

A classic trope is to falsely claim that transsexuals (or people in general) are telling kids that aren't trans in any fashion that they *are* in fact transgender or transsexual. They may also use emotionally loaded, sexualized language like "seduced" into being trans. (See classic trope of gay and lesbian people "recruiting", above.) One way of making it (falsely) seem especially evil is to claim that the kids being targeted have some special problem, a vulnerability that can be exploited (e.g. claim that the "victims" are autistic, have "untreated trauma", or have Borderline Personality Disorder), implying that these teens don't have self-agency. Please note, transsexuals are the LAST people who want other people to be living in a gender that doesn't suit them.

One of the ugliest strawman I've seen cast about is deliberately misconstruing the known high rate of depression and distress found in transkids who live in unsupportive environments is claiming that transkids 'blackmail' or 'manipulate' others by falsely threatening to commit suicide if they don't "get their way". The claim may be further amplified by stating that transkids (or transsexual adults) teach other transkids to use this threat. By making this claim, they paint transkids / adult transsexuals as manipulative monsters. Of course, this is actually an indication of their own lack of empathy and of their virulent hate. Shocking and impossible as this may seem, this claim really does make the rounds of social media.

Creating False Testimonials

One of the easiest ways that anti-trans propagandists can create a false testimonial is to claim a bogus hypothetical harm, *"If this transgender ideology had been around when I was a child, I would have been wrongly diagnosed as transgender."* This is typically claimed by a mildly gender-atypical woman, a "butch lesbian", but sometimes claimed by a typical heterosexual woman that liked to do a few "boy" things when young. Given that perhaps a third of women were somewhat "tomboyish", quite a few such transphobic women can make this false claim.

These false hypotheticals have the unique advantage that they can't be tested, challenged, or proven right or wrong. So they just exist, creating doubt, which is the goal.

Blaming Parents

An ugly, malicious, trope that has been around for years, especially from transphobic gays and lesbians, is that parents push their gender atypical, gay or lesbian, child or teen into falsely believing that they are transsexuals so that they won't be labeled gay or lesbian. The logic is twisted, but relies on the false notion that parents are more likely to be far more homophobic than transphobic. Ironically, many transkids actually experience the opposite; that transphobic parents, as they wrestle with their grief upon learning their child is transsexual, plead with their child to "*just*" be a CLOSETED gay or lesbian so that they, and their family, won't have to experience public embarrassment.

There is also the nasty lie that parents are abusing their children by "modifying their bodies". I've seen the lie that parents and doctors are prescribing such medications and conducting surgeries on pre-teens as young as three years old! No, that is NOT happening. No pre-teen is being given any medication (save possibly puberty blockers if they present with precocious puberty, which can and should be treated regardless of gender dysphoria).

Blaming Gender Clinics and Therapists

It has become fashionable to target specialized clinics that see gender atypical youth, especially in the UK, with false accusations. One also sees comments that call into question the membership, leadership, ethics, and Standards Of Care recommendations of WPATH, the leading professional society for those providing care for gender dysphoric individuals, just because *some* (but not a majority) of the members are transsexuals themselves. This is rather like dismissing the American Lung Society because some of its members survived lung cancer.

As some of these clinics have attracted new clients (not all of whom will persist), there is the hand-wringing over how rapidly the "epidemic" of gender issues has grown. Let's be real, going from zero to any number of clients is an infinitely large growth. Most clinics treating transkids are fairly new. Almost none are over twenty years old and most are less than ten.

We expect that an underserved market should respond with high growth when services become newly available.

If zero to something sounds too obvious, the propagandists pick another, but still early date to start, with the same seemingly startling growth. A common figure tossed about takes the form of 4400% which sounds really high... until one remembers that 100% = 2 times = double. So, 4400% growth is going from some really small number, say ten kids, when just opening such clinics, to 45 times that low starting number to make it only 450 kids (out of hundreds of thousands of kids in their multi-city/regional service area). But "4400%" sounds soooo much bigger and alarming!

The other way to make it sound really bad is to talk about how many children are REFERED to a clinic. But a referral does not mean that they were DIAGNOSED as being gender dysphoric... and it certainly doesn't mean that they are being tracked toward unnecessary medical treatment.

Another gambit is to point to transphobic medical providers who leave a given large institution because they have recently begun to provide services to transkids, as though it proved anything nefarious. But transphobic attitudes have always been found in the medical community, at about 50% (which is about the same number in the general public). Thus one expects to find such transphobic medical providers to jump ship as they find other employment and for propagandists to publicize it.

A more subtle propaganda gambit by anti-trans individuals and organizations is to describe themselves as merely concerned with "over medicalization" of gender variant youth. That sounds so reasonable, until one understands that ANY medical intervention is considered "over" medicalization by them.

A corollary false claim is that many teens are being prescribed hormones with no "medical oversight". That would constitute medical malpractice and as such is not likely to be common as doctors are as a group unlikely to risk that.

One of the lies put out is that therapists and clinics aren't providing full disclosure or "objective" advice. What they really mean is that the therapists aren't telling these kids and their parents what the transphobic people want them to tell them, including disinformation I discuss here. The simple truth is that the Standard of Care for all patients, gender dysphoric or not, is informed consent, giving full information, by both ethical and legal requirements. Claiming that these kids and their parents aren't being given this information is slander and libel.

A recent tactic is to claim that such clinics and therapists "never tell a kid that they are not trans" as though that was somehow nefarious, falsely implying that they are encouraging / pushing gender atypical youth to be transsexual and also falsely implying that they know which kids are 'true' transsexuals (or implying that no one is actually gender dysphoric) and who isn't. The real truth doesn't matter to them. There is no external test. No blood work, no magic words spoken in therapy. Only the individual, as they consider their own feelings and real life options, can make this determination and ultimately their life direction. No clinic or therapist, can from the outside, determine and say to anyone that they don't experience gender dysphoria.

Finally, there is the perennial threat to file lawsuits claiming malpractice for prescribing "unnecessary" medications or performing surgery on minors as a ploy to frighten caregivers away from serving the legitimate needs of transsexual youth. Consider this – how many such lawsuits have occured? I've never heard of even one such – have you? Certainly none that were successful. IF there had been, it would have made the news and would feature prominently in transphobic propaganda.

(Update: There is now exactly one legal case in Australia being touted by the transphobic press in which a woman is suing because she claims it is illegal to prescribe HRT to a teenager. Bets on when the case is thrown out as specious given that birth control is also HRT?)

(Update Oct. 2020: There is now a case in the UK which is trying to use the same argument that teenagers can't give consent, ignoring previous law granting those 16 years and over full consent rights and that no one is prescribing blockers to those under age 16 w/o parental consent.

Also note actual data on the so called "epidemic" of gender dysphoria, quoting from the article,

> *"Hyam told the court that referrals to GIDS had gone through a "twentyfold increase" from 97 in 2009 to 2,590 in 2018, and that the percentage of natal females had increased during that time and made up 76% of cases."*

So, going from when the clinic was barely started to today? At one of only two clinics in the entire UK? That's not an "epidemic".)

Creating Bogus Medical Societies

Doctors are not immune to bias and bigotry. Research has shown roughly half of doctors and psychologists are biased against LGBT people. So it would come as no surprise that a hateful minority ignore their professional duties to invest their time in creating alternative organizations specifically to create and spread false or misleading information about gender dysphoria. Some are part of older organizations, such as the tiny *American College of Pediatricians*, who historically attacked gay rights, pushed abusive 'therapies' to "cure" homosexuality and with it, transsexuality in children and teens. However, there is one very small band who specifically have targeted transsexuals and transkids, falsely and ironically naming themselves the *Society for Evidence Based Gender Medicine* whose members are notorious for spreading much of the anti-trans propaganda I list in this chapter.

Blaming Schools & Eductors

Schools are often the worst place for transkids, gay, lesbian, and bisexual youth and indeed anyone not in the majority in a given community. Bullying, most often by classmates, but all too often even by adults is a serious concern. That concern has been addressed by anti-bullying campaigns that may include empathy building by teaching youth in the school to be aware of and respect LGBT peers. But that has met with opposition from homophobic and transphobic parents and others. They decry that "Gender Ideology" is being taught in the schools. They demand that like sex education, it should be left to families, which in practice provide tacit approval for the continued bullying.

Another area of contention is access to gender appropriate bathrooms and changing facilities. Propagandists have seized this issue, looking to inflame the public with false stories or just insinuations that "boys will claim to be trans to molest girls in the locker room". Or worse, that MTF transkids ARE just boys who want to ogle girls in the locker room.

Just to be VERY clear. Gender dysphoric youth do NOT want to be seen naked by others of either sex. That's one of the key presenting symptoms of gender dysphoria in children and teens, extreme dislike and embarrassment of their sexed body. (This may or may not be true in adult / older transitioners / autogynephilic transsexuals, who have a very different form of 'gender dysphoria'.)

Therapy

In the past, it was near universal for therapy of gender atypical children, most often male, to mean attempts to "fix" them so that they were no longer gender atypical, as that was seen as a disorder in and of itself. It was also believed, falsely it turns out, that if they could get these boys to be gender typical in their behavior, they wouldn't develop into transsexuals or gay men. Therapies ranged from gentle "play" with a masculine role model to direct punishing and shaming children (up to and including corporal punishment; i.e. beatings) for atypicality on one hand and rewarding gender typicality on the other. Both philosophies encouraged parents to remove any and all cross-gender toys and activities, to deny cross-sex friendships, and to shame children, especially boys, for such play. Therapy for gender dysphoric teens was to "talk" them out of wanting to transition, usually by shaming them. Today such therapy, along with therapy meant to "talk" gay & lesbians out of being homosexual, is recognized as being both ineffective and abusive. Some states and countries have outlawed such practices. Professional societies of therapists and physicians have declared them to be unethical.

{Personal note: I was sent to play therapy as a ten-year old with Dr. Peters (you can't make this stuff up) a tall bearded man as a role model. While at home, my mother would jump down my throat if I so much as looked at a girl's toy. And at school, the teachers disrupted my friendships with girls and forced group activities with boys. Of course, that didn't work, so I was sent to talk therapy at 15/16, but knew enough not to talk about, nor answer his repeated questions about, neither my sexuality nor my gender behavior and identity so as to avoid any opportunity to shame me. Thus, I know about these practices first hand. Fortunately, in early 1975, at age 17, I was evaluated at the Stanford Gender Dysphoria Clinic which recommended social and medical transition. Unfortunately, my parents responded by kicking me out of the house.}

Today, most caring therapists and other caregivers recognize that gender atypicality is not in and of itself a disorder. They also recognize that most young mildly gender dysphoric children will desist on their own as they near adolescence, so there is no need for drastic measures either way.

However, extremely dysphoric children need outlets for their gender expression and that attempts to suppress or change their innate behavior is abusive and will only result in low self-esteem and shame.

They also know that such children need reassurance that they are loved by their parents. If punished for gender atypicality and/or expressing the pain of dysphoria, the bond between parent and child is put at grave risk. And yes, some therapists and their caring families recognize that some pre-adolescents and adolescents are better served by social transition.

This new kinder and gentler approach to gender atypicality and gender dysphoria has led to disinformation put out by those who wish that they could continue to offer abusive reparitive / conversion 'services', falsely claiming that such therapies do work. Some propagandists point to case history notes of reparitive therapists claim that their therapy is responsible for the 'resolution' of pre-adolescent gender dysphoria when in fact, they are falsely claiming credit for what is a natural process that would have happened without such abusive therapies. Transphobic parents and members of the public also lament this situation and put out the lie that "affirming" therapists are "forcing" gender atypical children and teens to become "transgender".

The basic truth is simple... just as it is not possible to "fix" LGBT people, it is not possible to force them to be LGBT against their nature. Saying otherwise is an outright lie.

Another tidbit of disinformation is claiming that therapists regularly "ok" teenagers to get hormones with only one visit. In over four decades of experience and discussions with literally... oh I can't even guess the number of transfolk of all ages I've met or corresponded with. It would have to be the hundreds now, the fastest I've ever heard of for someone to get their "letter" approving HRT from a psych professional was five one hour sessions. And when others hear of that low figure, they are incredulous because most adults were required to have at least several months of weekly sessions and most had more, some over a year or more. There's a reason why therapists and psychiatrists are called "gatekeepers". For minors, it might be faster to get onto puberty blockers if they are seen in longer more intense sessions with at least one second opinion since the clock is seen as "ticking", but to switch from blockers, or for an older teen, one already past puberty? That will take longer.

{Personal Note: I was that teenager who had only five hours in 1975, a record even for the Stanford Gender Dysphoria Clinic: three one hour sessions alone, one hour with my mother, and one hour with my father. And no, I have no real idea why I got my letter with so few visits, but if I had to guess, it was because I still had to wait until I was 18 because my parents refused permission... and that I had previously been in therapy that had been anything but "affirming". Interestingly, when I was 23 and had the funds for surgery, the surgeon, a private doc in Colorado, required two recent "letters" from psychiatrists. I had six one hour sessions with one psychiatrist and one hour for the second opinion... this too was considered a record. This one I did know why... emotional maturity, intelligence, and five solid years post social transition with a great work and education history.}

Social Transition

I see over and over claims that merely allowing a child to cross-dress or socially transition is a form of "child abuse" in and of itself. I've even seen transphobes complaining that letting non-transkids know that transkids and transadults exist and should be accepted and respected, is a form of child abuse! These claims are usually from the most virulently transphobic and homophobic members of the public. However, there is a more subtle form of this parental shaming in that people claim that because many pre-teens who are gender atypical will not be gender dysphoric, that they are "forcing" their kids to be "transgender". This meme even floats in the gay and lesbian community claiming that parents do this because they are homophobic and would rather have a transsexual child than a gay or lesbian one(!). My own experience has indicated that homophobic parents are universally also transphobic, so the logic of this assertion is faulty and groundless.

Parents should be advised that many pre-teens who are gender atypical will in truth grow up to be gay or lesbian. Given this, loving parents should be open to listening to the needs of their children as they grow up and be flexible in their hopes.

A recent meme making the rounds is that if a child is allowed to cross-dress as a pre-teen, to use a new name etc. they will have social and personal difficulty later when they desist from being gender dysphoric. Some go as far as to say that this will cause them trauma, having spent years growing up presenting as the "wrong sex". But this only shows their own transphobic bias, valuing the lives and welfare of desisting children over persisting transkids. Consider this from the viewpoint of persisting transkids, if having to grow up presenting as the "wrong sex" is traumatic and that transitioning is a social and personal difficulty at that later age, won't these kids have had a similarly bad experience if they are not allowed to socially transition earlier? Either both are true or neither is true. Actually, the truth is that children who will desist later are still in pain now. And desisting children detransitioning is no more traumatic than either type transitioning in the first place. But the transphobic propagandists aren't interested in nuance and dealing with things in such a way as to reduce pain for everyone on a day-to-day basis. Remember this. Their goal is not to help your child be happy and emotionally healthy. They are only interested in frightening the parents of transkids into NOT allowing them to socially transition in the hope that denying them this at a young age will force them to not get puberty blockers, which will them force them to endure a puberty which will make it that much more difficult for them to transition successfully as adults, which will keep them from being *one of those people*".

A more subtle and insidious bit of propaganda is to point out that in speaking of the likely hood of a child desisting or persisting that a pre-adolescent social transition "predicts" persistence. The sneaky part is, while there is a correlation between such a pre-adolescent social transition and persistence, the way that the word "predicts" is interpreted is one of causation rather than merely being a successful test of the level of gender dysphora that already exists and the natural affinity / social comfort that a child experiences post social transition. That is to say, attempting social transition is a great diagnostic test that persistors will take to like a duckling takes to water, while desistors are likely to find social transition does not help them.

One of the ugly issues I've seen thrown around is that of impugning the motives and values of various researchers and clinicians, on both sides of the issue of pre-teen transition. Most professionals have nothing but good intentions. Each has nuanced views because this issue is not black and white. But many insist that it should be black and white... and thus will smear those who don't agree with their own position.

After the age of twelve, social transition is, or at least should be, a no-brainer. If a teen was gender atypical and dysphoric as a preteen, their desire and need for social transition is one that they should decide for themselves. In fact, attempting to socially transition is a great "test" since if it doesn't help them, it will be an obvious fact.

Surgery

Perhaps the most common propaganda seen bandied about is the oldest. In the mid-50s, as the public began to learn about transsexuality and its medical treatment, many were quick to note that "there is no such thing as a sex change", as though that proved something profoundly debunking. Well, this is both a true and yet misleading statement. It is true in that no surgery, then or now, can take a fertile individual of one sex and result in a fertile member of the other sex. What is misleading is that the goal of surgery was never fertility, but palliative. It is to allow individuals who suffer, and suffer greatly, from somatic gender dysphoria to inhabit a body that approximates that of the opposite sex to a close enough degree that it alleviates their dysphoria. Although many transsexuals would love to be fertile in their new gender, they are willing to accept this trade-off to enable a good enough life.

A common ploy is to point out that surgeons are paid to perform these procedures and are "getting rich", insinuating that they are evil and greedy. I do hope those that say this never need a lifesaving operation so that they won't have to pay an evil and greedy surgeon.

A very common ploy is to paint medical interventions as "destroying healthy bodies", totally disregarding the emotional pain of gender dysphoria as worthy of medical treatment. The underlying message that they are trying to implant is that there was no medical necessity, and thus it was monstrous to treat it. But consider that nearly no one bats an eye when women have breast augmentation, rhinoplasty (cosmetic nose surgery), or even that there is no medical reason for the vast majority of male circumcisions (genital surgery) that baby boys are subjected to years before they can give informed consent.

Some people will point out that SRS sterilizes transsexuals as though that were in and of itself medical malpractice, even incorrectly invoking the Hippocratic oath "to do no harm". This is a puzzling attitude since many medical issues are treated in such a way that also results in sterilization and no one calls that malpractice. In fact, many healthy men and women chose voluntary permanent sterilization which is an accepted practice. For young adults (even if under the age of 18) to knowingly make the trade-off of continuing to suffer somatic gender dysphoria vs. accepting voluntary sterilization is a personal choice for them and them alone to make.

The next bit of propaganda is to describe the result of surgery as ugly, monstrous, or diseased to invoke visceral disgust. Mary Daly, an extremely transphobic author in the 1970's described post-operative transsexuals as "Frankenstein's Monsters", invoking the image of people hacked together by rogue mad scientist doctors. Other comments focus on and exaggerate the potential for surgical complications. Very recentlyI've seen an outright lie repeated and amplified in social media in which the result of Male-To-Female transsexual surgery is an "open wound" which is easily "infected", rather than a functional neo-vagina. What loving parent would want their child to experience such iatrogenic trauma?

A more subtle bit of misleading disinformation is to combine the two memes above, to describe the result of MTF surgery as taking functional male genitalia and turning it into "dysfunctional male genitalia" in an attempt to invoke disgust on one hand and parental concern for their child's future happiness on the other. The lie depends upon parents not being familiar with the cosmetic nor functional results because, let's face it, that's not something to be bragged about in public. So, I will attempt here, while remaining within socially acceptable bounds, to answer that, given that I myself have such "dysfunctional male genitalia"... Ummmm... well... I'm VERY happily married to a straight man... and neither of us is unhappy with the results... 'nough said.

Another reason these particular talking points work is that parents hang onto the false hope that their child will desist and be heterosexual. While it is true that pre-teens who are gender atypical but not particularly dysphoric are more likely to desist than persist, such boys will most likely grow up to be gay, the girls may or may not be lesbian, given that many tomboyish girls are mislabeled as gender atypical. These tomboyish girls will most likely grow up to be straight. However, those teens who had been gender atypical AND notably gender dysphoric as pre-teens will not likely desist after age twelve. Besides, one doesn't perform surgery on pre- or even early teens. One is required to wait until the late teens at the earliest and by then, it's pretty obvious that surgery is right for those who know the trade-offs... and rationally chose to exchange genitalia which they will never use for those that they will joyfully use.

Another bugbear thrown around is the specter of post-operative regret. I won't lie in turn; this is a real phenomena. However, what is not often discussed in the parental fora is that the vast majority of those who later regret SRS are "late onset" autogynephiles. These are usually males who have successfully lived as adult men, very often married to women, fathering children, etc. They previously had extensive sexual experience as men, enjoying their 'original equipment'. In female individuals, gender dysphoria that first present in adolescence has been associated with later detransitioning and regret, but in fewer individuals and certainly far fewer than in the public imagination. (I'm referring to actual gender dysphoric individuals, not those girls who falsely claim a 'trans' or 'non-binary' identity.) Post operative regret is nearly absent from "early onset" transsexuals. And those few who were regretful weren't regretting the loss of their 'original equipment' but complained of the rare complications that may occur with any surgery.

For parents of Female-to-Male (FtM) teens and twenty-somethings, there is often fear that "top surgery" to remove/reduce unwanted breasts will be regretted as well. This fear is especially potent in the mothers of FtM transkids because of the natural empathy one feels, of putting themselves into their child's position and feeling angst at the thought of the loss of their own breasts. Of course, this is putting their own shoes onto their child, instead of walking a bit in theirs.

There has been a recent blitz of disinformation and propaganda about FtM transmen chest binding being "harmful" with little to no clinical evidence. But consider that this binding provides no more flattening / compression, and indeed often far less compression of the ribcage and internal organs, than many feminine fashion undergarments in recent history such as corsets, girdles, etc. I've even seen binding being described as 'barbaric' and likened to Female Genital Mutilation. Except, no one is forcing transmen to bind. Also, transmen are likely not concerned with any alleged harm to breasts that they revile and expect to surgically remove. Finally, I have to point out that no one seems to be upset about pre-op transwomen "tucking", which would seemingly come closer to the description of "genital mutilation". This is likely because the anti-chest-binding lobby is mostly lesbian whose natural, if misapplied, sympathy is for female bodied gynephilic people (which most transmen are) and have very little sympathy, and often great antipathy, for transwomen.

Puberty Blockers

One egregious lie that I've seen bandied about, even by physicians, is that puberty blockers cause permanent sterility, often with the misleading term "chemical castration". They do not. In fact, that was the whole point of puberty blockers, to reversibly delay the onset of puberty and its effects to allow young teens some time to emotionally mature before making more permanent changes in the course of their sexual maturation. Without such blockers, their bodies will make the decision for them... and this may be very much against their wishes (it certainly was against mine!). Cessation of the blockers allows the natal puberty to resume, with no loss of fertility, unless other medical intervention is begun (such as cross-sex hormones).

Some commenters falsely assert that puberty blocking is dangerous and experimental, often going so far as to profess that doctors who prescribe it and parents who allow it should be imprisoned. They fail to note that puberty blocking has become a standard of care for precocious puberty and that the medications used are FDA approved for blocking puberty. Thus this is NOT "experimental" nor any more dangerous than many other medically indicated prescriptions.

The next level of insidious misinformation is to claim that such medication hasn't been specifically "approved" for gender dysphoric kids. This is a fantastic Catch-22 because no matter how long it's been standard practice, it will NEVER be so listed by the FDA because to do so, the drug company would have to spend huge amounts of money to conduct the study, which they have no need nor incentive to do; Gender dysphoric transkids are a tiny minority and not worth a drug company's notice.

For instance, a cancer drug that was studied and approved in colon cancer that is later discovered to treat skin cancer would not need to be specifically 'approved' for that use. Doctors would simply prescribe it "off label", a well-established and legal practice, as long as it meets established standards of care in the profession.

Use of puberty blockers is an established and recommended practice in this field.

Then, I read a whopper on social media that one can't use the safety and efficacy data from precocious puberty studies with transkids. Wow! Who knew that transkids respond to medications differently than non-gender dysphoric children? Are they a different species? Seriously, one has to take much of this kind of propaganda with a sense of humor.

One misleading claim I've seen on social media is that puberty blockers interfere with brain development. This has not been found. But it certainly sounds scary, which is the real intent of making the claim.

Another outrageous lie that I've seen recently is the assertion that Lupron (puberty blocker) directly causes suicide. I guess if one is going to lie, one may as well make it a whopper. Depression is unfortunately common and people who are prescribed Lupron as adults are often under severe stress due to their underlying illness, typically terminal cancer, leading to reports of depression.

To be clear, there is NO reported direct association between puberty blockers and depression / suicidal ideation in transkids. However, if a child who is extremely gender atypical and dysphoric experiences negative social and familial attitudes, that may be an independent source of stress leading to depression.

A very recent bit of wild lie is to say that "thousands have died on Lupron" insinuating that it was the cause of their deaths. The truth is that these adults died of prostate or other cancers and were taking Lupron as treatment to slow (not stop) the cancer.

I've also seen a rather strange assertion that having been on puberty blockers then switching to cross-hormone replacement therapy somehow leaves the child in a prepubescent state. In the sense that the child won't experience the changes that would have occurred had they not been on blockers, namely for natal females breast development or for natal males, enlargement of the penis and testicles, voice deepening, beard growth, along with increased upper body strength, this assertion is true... and indeed is the desired effect. So why the strange assertion that this is somehow a problem? The meme is also sending the false message that somehow the child will remain forever looking like a prepubescent child, never to appear to be as a sexually mature adult. The fact remains that cross-sex HRT will allow the child to mature with all of the cross-sex secondary sexual characteristics in a manner closely approximating that of the opposite sex which is, after all, the goal.

In a bid to create confusion and doubt, one recent meme I've seen, mixed in the usual disinformation, is that taking puberty blockers will leave MTF transkids with a penis that is "too small" to form a proper 'inversion' neo-vagina. This is of course an effort to convince parent to refuse blockers so that their child will suffer all the damaging effects of a masculinizing puberty and fail to pass successful later. They don't actually care if transgirls have big enough vaginas for comfortable sex as adults. Just to be clear, decades of transkids who have had successful SRS surgeries, etc. after having been on HRT from a very early age put the lie to this absurd meme. Not to be too indelicate, but the inverted skin is very easily stretched over time, from both dilation and from coitus (as I know very well from personal experience). Another factor that this meme fails to take into account is that even if we could fabricate a blocker that allows genital growth while eliminating all other unwanted effects of a masculinizing puberty, the genital growth in and of itself will dramatically increase gender dysphoric trauma and should itself be avoided.

Perhaps the most bizarre bit of misinformation is that somehow, if an MTF transkid doesn't go through the typical natal male puberty to sexually mature, they will never be able to experience sexual satisfaction. While testosterone does cause human male brains to develop at puberty, estrogen and micronized progesterone, both part of HRT protocols, will do much the same. In fact, though never published, there is very strong anecdotal evidence that MTF transkids experience very strong libido development on natural estrogen (E2) compared to other sources (e.g. premarin or estinyl-estradiol). If you think about it for a moment, this makes sense... given that women have sexual drives as much as men do... and they never went through a male puberty!

It could be argued (and indeed I have so argued), that it would be better to switch from puberty blockers to HRT earlier than some clinicians insist upon waiting, so that the final results are better and so that the teens will appear to be maturing on the same schedule as their peers, for better social functioning. There are also concerns about bone strength later in life which may be impacted by extended use of puberty blockers. This is an argument for earlier HRT, NOT against the use of puberty blockers.

Moreover, I've seen a very clever bit of misdirection suggesting that MTF transkids, when they begin HRT bone density "fails to catch up" (oh dear!). Fails to catch up with whom we should ask, but they don't tell us that they don't catch up with BOYS, who have larger bones. These MTF transkids don't want to "catch up" with boys, they want their bones to be female-like so that they can pass as typical girls, not big lumbering boys.

One of the most illogical arguments I've seen against the use of puberty blockers is twisting the statistics that most transkids who go on puberty blockers will persist and require HRT and perhaps surgery... as though being on puberty blockers caused them to persist (!). This is a failure to note that desisters do so before puberty. The fact that most persisters in puberty who go on blockers continue to be gender dysphoric is a non-causal correlation, in the same sense that taking antibiotics during infections does not mean that antibiotics caused the infection! The fact is that persisters who are unable to obtain blockers or HRT at that age will also remain gender dysphoric and will seek out and obtain HRT at a later age (either on the street or legally when they reach majority as I did). Refusing to provide blockers or HRT in puberty will not increase the rate of desistance but will increase the need for more medical / cosmetic interventions later on (e.g. mastectomy / electrolysis) and likely leave such an individual "funny looking" as an adult (e.g. wide hips on a transman, androgynous face and low pitched voice on a transwoman).

A recent lie I've seen is to talk about parents putting their children on puberty blockers as early as age eight (or even age six in one recent agit prop piece in the Federalist !!!) (age five in Breitbart – they keep pushing the age down)(Wow! Age three in another Breitbart piece). Of course, this was a deliberate distortion of the truth that some children ARE placed on puberty blockers at age eight or nine. But

NOT because they are gender dysphoric, but because they have precocious puberty. These children are on puberty blockers because entering a precocious puberty at age eight or nine is not good for their long term health, regardless of whether they are gender dysphoric or not, and most children placed on blockers at such a young age are NOT gender dysphoric.

One argument I've seen against the use of puberty blockers for MTF transkids is that they shouldn't be started until she has stored sperm in a sperm bank for later use! This one is a true head twister, as that would require a transgirl to undergo an unwanted, physically and emotionally devastating masculinizing puberty, by which time, blockers are metaphorically shutting the barn doors, too late to do their intended job. The argument also completely misrepresents transgirls who will grow up to be transwomen. Early onset MTF transkids are universally exclusively sexually and romantically attracted to straight men. Storing sperm? To what end? So that they can use it to impregnate their future wives?!?! That's the definition of unclear on the concept. Transgirls will grow up to marry men. And if they and their husbands chose to build a family with the aid of a gestational surrogate, they will use their husband's sperm. (Can you imagine the damaging psychological issues raised by suggesting that one use a transwoman's stored sperm, for both partners?)

Finally, I've seen comparisons of using puberty blockers by teens to NAZI medical experiments in concentration camps. When such hyperbole is invoked, one knows it is propaganda.

Hormone Replacement Therapy

The most common bit of propaganda about hormones is that their use will be "life long" as though that was somehow an evil in its own right to be avoided at all costs (even including living a life of unhappy gender dysphoria and social awkwardness).

To make a personal digression, swallowing a few pills each day has never been a major issue for me these past four decades and some. Far more impactful in my own life is the fact that I've been dependent upon asthma medication since I was five years old, medication which has far more harsh side effects (theophylline caused insomnia for years, rescue inhalers cause the heart to race and the lungs to itch uncomfortably, steroid inhalers increase the risk of fungus infection in the mouth and throat... and if the meds fail to control the asthma, a trip to the emergency room is needed or one could die, no joke) and far more expensive.

Those who have diabetes are similarly dependent 'life long' upon insulin, a life saving medication.

However, forgetting to take one's hormones for a short period of time is NOT life threatening, nor even very uncomfortable. A few weeks of not taking them, if one has not had their gonads removed, they will begin to produce steroids again. If they have had their gonads removed, they may experience 'hot flashes'. While not comfortable, they are not life threatening. The greatest danger is the potential risk for osteoporosis. But this an increase in the risk, not a certainty.

A number of individuals point to HRT as being inherently dangerous, increasing the risk of blot clots, etc. These risks are no greater than girls taking birth control pills and if one is seriously worried about it, one can simultaneously take baby aspirin as a blood thinner. A recent study showed that estradiol, today's preferred protocol, had NO increased risk of blood clots.

Another bit of propaganda is to grossly exaggerate the risk of breast cancer from estrogen. However, with decades of HRT use by transsexuals, we have only seen a small handful of cases which were certainly NOT indicative of increased risk compared to natal females. In fact, the risk seemed to be at about 30% lower than natal females. But is higher than natal males who were not transsexual. (Yes, men get breast cancer too.)

Interestingly, the risk of some cancers is significantly reduced in transsexuals due to surgery and HRT. For example, top surgery reduces the risk of breast cancer prophylactically. Radical hysterectomy (as part of 'bottom surgery') eliminates the risk of ovarian cancer and endometriosis. For MTF folk, SRS eliminates the risk of testicular cancer and reduces the risk of prostate cancer, as does HRT itself.

As well as claiming risks of cancer, I've seen outright lies that HRT causes mental illness!

We've heard stories of young transmen being discouraged from taking testosterone because it "shortens" lives. This is based on the statistical fact that men have lower life expectancies. However, they fail to note that most of those deaths occur early in life, as male children are more likely to die than female. Then, there is the increased death rate among young men due to violence and misadventure. Finally, males carry only one X chromosome, so if there is a bad gene on it, they won't have the extra copy to compensate. Combined, all of these issues lead to men having a lower life expectancy, none of which are mediated by testosterone.

On the other hand, it is known that castrated males do live slightly longer. So by this logic, all men should be medically castrated as teenagers!

Another gambit is to point to a couple studies that show that estrogen "causes cognitive deficits" in MTF transfolk, specifically reducing their mental rotational abilities, while also saying that testosterone reduces FTM transfolk's verbal fluency. The HORROR, HRT causes mental problems! Actually, what they are measuring is the very tiny subtle differences already found in men and women in which men are very *slightly* better, on average, than women at mentally rotating three dimensional figures and women are very *slightly* better, on average, than men at verbal fluency. These turn out to be influenced by hormones in the brain, so no surprise that they should influence transsexual on HRT. But the effect is so small as to be almost impossible to detect in any one individual.

I think the silliest claim I've heard is that "Big Pharma" is pushing the diagnoses of gender dysphoria so that they can sell more hormones. Given that gender dysphoria is extremely rare... but even if it is silly on the face of it, officials in the UK actually investigated that claim and debunked it.

Parents deserve accurate information, not propaganda and lies —
from either

ABOUT THE AUTHOR

Candice H. Brown Elliott uses the pen name "Kay Brown" to write about transsexual and transgender science, history, and politics. She writes science fiction novels under the pen name of "Seaby Brown". She and her husband Jeff live in an historic house as empty nesters where they both write extensively. Candice's two foster/adopt children are now adult.

Candice's blog on transsexual science may be found at https://sillyolme.wordpress.com

Her twitter account is @display_geek